DAILY THOUGHTS ON
Living Free

D1516249

DAILY THOUGHTS ON
Living Free

NEVA COYLE

BETHANY HOUSE PUBLISHERS
MINNEAPOLIS, MINNESOTA 55438
A Division of Bethany Fellowship, Inc.

Published by Bethany House Publishers
A Division of Bethany Fellowship, Inc.
6820 Auto Club Road, Minneapolis, Minnesota 55438

Printed in the United States of America

Library of Congress Cataloging in Publication Data

Coyle, Neva, 1943-
   Daily thoughts on living free.

   1. Devotional calendars.   I. Title.
BV4811.C685   242'.2   82-4495
ISBN 0-87123-286-3   AACR2

About the Author

NEVA COYLE, founder and president of Overeaters Victorious, lives in California with her husband and three children. Educated in California and Minnesota, she attended Rasmussen School of Business and Lakewood Community College. She is traveling much of the time on speaking engagements and her "Free To Be Thin" Seminars.

Other books by Neva Coyle

Free To Be Thin, co-authored with Marie Chapian
Free To Be Thin Study Guide No. 1, Getting Started
Free To Be Thin Study Guide No. 2, Discipline
Living Free, Neva's own true story of deliverance and victory
    in her everyday life.
Scriptures for Living Free, a ring-bound compilation of scrip-
    tures, illustrated, and designed for display on desk or
    countertop, to be used as a companion volume to *Daily
    Thoughts on Living Free*.

Contents

Introduction

What do we do when faced with temptation? Struggle, resist, try to think about something else? Rebuke Satan with shallow words, scream (aloud or silently)? Cry, pout, or complain?

Actually, there is a very simple solution. Not always easy, but simple. When faced with temptation, our only weapon of warfare is the Word of God. When Jesus was approached by Satan with his unholy proposals, Jesus used the *Word*. Notice that He did not use random selections of scripture, but the appropriate Word related to the temptation.

In this book, I have written about the practical, everyday happenings of life, and applied the appropriate Word of God. The Word of God can help us in every situation; it can change us into mighty warriors ready to meet every battle, and win. The Word of God can meet your needs when you oppose Satan in the kitchen, coffee shop, grocery store, PTA meeting or department store. It can bring you back to your right standing as a winner instead of a loser; it can lift you from depression into joy, from fatigue into energy. You can use the Word and win. But you do have to use it.

To use the Word of God you will need to speak it aloud when facing the tempter—the accuser—and he will actually flee from you. It is great to have the power of the Word of God; to depend on the flesh is to fail, for it is weak. The Word of God is your offensive weapon. Get on out there and fight! You will win!

This book contains fifty-two devotionals, to be used once a week as an alternate with other devotional material, or on a daily basis, if you prefer. The worksheets will help you to sort out what the Lord is saying to you through His Word. Each devotional will help you to apply the Word of God in a practical way, and see it work in your own circumstances.

If you already have an established quiet time as a regular part of your daily routine, this book will fit right in and you are ready to begin. If you have not been having a daily quiet time with the Lord, you will need to establish a time and a place to do so. By the time you have finished this book, the quiet time will be part of you, you will realize the importance of it, and won't ever want to be without it again.

I trust that this book will be a blessing to you, just as writing it has blessed me.

Romans Reinforcements

Do you ever need to be reinforced? What does it mean? Webster defines it as—

1. To give more force or effectiveness, to "strengthen," support.

2. To strengthen with additional manpower or equipment (military).

3. To strengthen as by adding extra support or padding.

Think about an old black-and-white Western movie— where the good guy wears a white hat and the bad guy wears a black hat. The good guys are surrounded by bad guys in a blazing gun battle. The good guys are exhausted. The hero pulls the trigger twice in rapid succession, but all you hear is the click, click of the empty chamber—he has just fired his last bullet! Now what? The ragtime-style piano sounds out the mood. The faces of the good guys reflect despair and certain defeat. But wait . . . off in the distance . . . the faint sound of a bugle can be heard. A little louder now, and we all cheer at the sight of dust clouds and the sound of pounding hoofs. The bugle call sounds again. The hoofbeats are stronger—it's the Cavalry! Hooray! The hero now takes on the bad guys hand to hand. He finds new energy and determination. Why? He has hope of reinforcement.

Now think about your daily life. Could you use a Cavalry? Could you do with a little reinforcement?

Romans is just such a reinforcement. You can refer to these mighty words and phrases whenever you need help, when you feel surrounded by "bad guys," when you feel that you have fired your last bullet. When certain defeat or failure are at hand, you can be reinforced with the Word of God.

As you read, remember that you are placing within your spirit the very reinforcement that you will need to go through the day victoriously.

Think of it as a football game. To make the goal you will have to push the opposing team back a long way. You will need these effective reinforcements. They have been a help to me when I have needed them most. God's Word is the one sure thing on which we can rely. Use it. It will reinforce you in ways you didn't dream possible.

Living in Christ

Romans 6:6

Do you ever feel as though you are not making any progress toward your goal of what you would like to be? Does the weight loss seem like an unending battle? Does your housework seem to be a constant struggle for organization? Do you still succumb to old patterns and habits that you want to be rid of?

Romans 6:6 tells us that the old, unrenewed self was nailed to the cross with Jesus. It tells us that we are not to consider ourselves slaves to the appetites of the flesh any longer.

Let me tell you about Nora.

I met Nora at a retreat. She was 150 pounds overweight. She was unattractive, lonely, confused, and you could tell by her appearance that she did not think too highly of herself. But Nora accepted Jesus as her Savior at that retreat. She was soon filled with the Holy Spirit—she was transformed by the love and miraculous power of God. I recently received a letter from her:

> *"Dear Neva, I just want you to know that every day I thank God that Overeaters Victorious came into my life. Also, that God gave me a beautiful spiritual sister, Dee. There are times when old Satan almost gets the best of me, but I call Dee, and receive help through the Scriptures. She reminds me what Jesus has done for me.*
>
> *I know that I wouldn't have lost 120 pounds without Him. (I still have 30 more to lose to reach my goal.) It's been a lot slower toward the end, but the Lord is dealing with me about thoughts that are potentially destructive to my body as well as my mind. Scripture has been my guide, and often I just sing for joy; it is such a blessing.*
>
> *Neva, I can't stop talking about how great God is. I*

would be an evangelist if I could. I have stopped people on the street and told them that Jesus loves them.

Keep on doing God's work. I pray that God will provide all your needs to keep you going to reach people like me.

I recently bought a size 14 pants from a friend. Do you remember that when I came into OV I had a friend that made all my clothes? She used a size 26¹/₂ pattern an then added onto it. So, you see? That's why I can't keep my mouth shut! Praise God!"

What a wonderful illustration of Romans 6:6. Nora is truly renewed. She is not even a shadow of her former self. She has been transformed—born again. She has become a new creation. It has not always been a high road for Nora—she has battled with cancer twice through her time of weight loss. She came to see me once and said, "Jesus is the answer! He is in complete control. I will simply trust Him for this problem as I have learned to trust Him for every other problem."

Won't you take this encouragement from Nora today? Let Jesus prove himself to you. Take Him as your personal Savior and then experience Him in a mighty way in your life. Not everyone's story will be as dramatic as Nora's, but a miracle is still miraculous. Nora's story may not be your story, but let yours be written. Let God move in your life in a way you never thought or dreamed possible. Living with and for Jesus is not a life of sacrifice, it is a life full of living, with Him, for Him, by Him.

It's *living free!*

"We know that our old (unrenewed) self was nailed to the cross with Him in order that [our] body, [which is the instrument] of sin, might be made ineffective and inactive for evil, that we might no longer be the slaves of sin." Romans 6:6.

God is saying to me:

Thoughts I'm having today:

I've shared with the Lord:

Further thoughts and prayers:

Quiet Times

Romans 6:16

There is a cake on the table, left there by one of the members of your family. You have just come in from a strenuous period of exercise and you are feeling like you need a quick-energy pick-me-up. The cake begins to call your name; the refrigerator begins to speak to you, listing all the items it contains; the cupboard door flies open and proudly displays its wares. From somewhere you hear the coaxing of temptation, and it sounds logical:

"You deserve a break today; just a little treat won't hurt. Who would know? You can always diet tomorrow." You feel your resolve dissolve. Your determination is lagging.

Now is the time to declare God's Word! Your quiet times fortify you for such times as these.

You *are* having your quiet times, aren't you? Early, when the house is quiet, pick up the Bible and let God speak to you; then you speak to Him. You will find encouragement for the day. He wants to lead you from bondage into freedom.

Choosing obedience requires active participation on your part. Repeating God's Word aloud is an effective tool. It is an offensive weapon to be used in times of temptation, discouragement and doubt.

In the book of Nehemiah we read of a great restoration project undertaken to rebuild the walls of the city of Jerusalem. The walls had been overrun and at least partially destroyed by the enemy, leaving the city without this vital defense. The people lived in constant danger because of the damage to the wall. As I studied this section of Scripture, I realized that as a Christian, I have at times had the walls of defense broken down in my life also. When I was actively seeking God for insight into my overeating problem, I saw that my walls of defense were down. This section of the Bible held many keys for me as I took on the project of rebuilding these walls.

I found in the fourth chapter that one way to overcome the threats of the enemy, as I was rebuilding my "wall," was to be constantly prepared to face him by having my tools in one hand and my weapon in the other.

In Ephesians, chapter 6, we find the description of the Christian's armor, with our offensive weapon being the Word of God.

Let me illustrate:

Before going into the corner grocery store to pick up a few necessary items for the family, I take the time to recite Romans 6:16. This is my weapon, remember, and yours as well. My response to the passage is this: "I do not let sin rule as king in my body to make me yield to its cravings. I am not subject to its lusts and evil passions. I do not offer or yield my bodily members to overeating but offer and yield myself to God. I have been raised from deathly habits to perpetual life. I present my body and its members to God as implements of righteousness."

I go into the store with my sword held high, and meditating on this verse I have the strength to pass up all the goodies that otherwise would tempt me.

The Word further prompts me to confess: "I surrender and yield my appetite as an instrument of obedience to the Lord. I do not surrender to the demands of the flesh. I choose to be obedient to the Word of God. I crucify the flesh. The flesh is dead."

You can rebuild your wall of defense using God's Word. Pick up your weapon and use it offensively, not just defensively. You will win! God is ready to help you as you learn about *living free.*

> *"Do you not know that if you continually surrender yourselves to any one to do his will, you are the slaves of him whom you obey, whether that be to sin, which leads to death, or to obedience which leads to righteousness—right doing and right standing with God?"*
> *Romans 6:16*

God is saying to me:

Thoughts I'm having today:

I've shared with the Lord:

Further thoughts and prayers:

Rewards

Romans 6:22

Did you ever vacuum the floor, and then reward yourself with a piece of cake and a cup of coffee? I have done this very thing. When I woke up to the fact, it changed my life. Let me share it with you:

One day I read Romans chapter 6, verse 22: "But having been freed from sin and enslaved to God, you derive your benefit, resulting in sanctification, and the outcome, eternal life." (NAS)

These words called my attention to the fact that everything I could possibly want, that really matters in the light of eternity, is mine. What a trap I was in, of having to reward myself for the common, ordinary tasks of life. Did I seek rewards in other areas of my life as well? I began to observe my motives more closely.

I noticed that I selected the clothes that would be noticed by my friends, and draw compliments. I couldn't go to the laundromat without first applying my makeup perfectly, just in case I met someone I knew. (I didn't want anyone to say that I looked less than spectacular.) I needed the reward of compliments. I don't mean to say that you should not take some thought as to how you look when you go to the laundromat, but there are times when clean and neat suffice and "spectacular" is not necessary. There are times and circumstances for the way we dress and appear. When we live life centered around what others like, feel, and say, we lose touch with our own identity.

If I cleaned out the closet, I made sure that my husband saw it as soon as he returned from work. When I thoroughly cleaned my house, I threw a party, and when I made a new dress, I wore it at the very first opportunity. A freshly baked cake had to be displayed on the table; a job at church had to be a visible project. Everything I did carried some reward.

Consequently, I lived for the approval of others. But where

did that leave me? If no one ever saw the closet, would that mean I should not organize it? Didn't it make a difference to me if the closet was neat? Of course it did.

Everyone had always said that I looked good in blue, so I responded by filling my closet with an almost exclusive blue wardrobe. But what about my preferences for pink, peach, green, and gray? My friends didn't do this to me. I did!

This brought me to the question, "What if there is no reward, no cake, no compliments! Where do I get the strength to do what I know to do without this reinforcement?" From God's Word! I discovered that when I meditated on His Word, it gave me the strength to do everything I needed to do in this temporal life, without the necessity of everyone's approval.

I am an eternal being, created by God—I am a follower of Jesus. I am an individual with purpose. It's not what I get from life, but who I am, that makes the difference.

So go to it today! Count your calories; vacuum your floor; do all that you have put off until now because it was not rewarding—not for what you will get, but because of who you are. The reward is *living free.*

"But now since you have been set free from sin and become the slaves of God, you have your present reward in holiness and its end is eternal life." Romans 6:22

God is saying to me:

Thoughts I'm having today:

I've shared with the Lord:

Further thoughts and prayers:

Inner Strength

Romans 7:6

It's late in the day. You must stop at the store for that loaf of bread and milk for the family. You have made this trip before, and you are aware of the temptations you will face. The trip from the dairy case to the cash register is lined on both sides from floor to over your head with items designed to appeal to your impulsive/compulsive nature.

You sit in the car, and contemplate the confrontation ahead of you. You had such a good quiet time this morning, and you fed on God's Word until you felt saturated with His presence. But it has been a busy day—you have been faced with all kinds of pressures at work, and you are exhausted. The dinner hour is still ahead of you, and the long evening (the hardest part of the day for an overeater). You feel as if you cannot make it without some little pick-me-up.

This is the time to be on the alert! Logic can come in and spoil your quality decisions to live a life of self-control and discipline. Now is the time to rely on the Word of God. Speak to your body the Words that give life!

Romans, chapters 7 and 8, have verses that contain life-giving truths. Get out your Bible and review them: "I discern in my bodily members, in the sensitive appetites and wills of the flesh, the law at war against the law of my mind, trying to make me a prisoner to the law of sin that wants to dominate and rule my body. But since I live after the dictates of the spirit, and not the dictates of the flesh, I will experience no condemnation. My life is governed not by the dictates of the the flesh, but I am controlled instead by the dictates of the Holy Spirit.

"I am a debtor, it is true. But not to the flesh. I am not obligated to my carnal nature, I don't have to live a life ruled by the standards set up by the dictates of the flesh.

"I surrender and yield my appetite as an instrument of obedience to the Lord. I do not surrender to the demands of the flesh. I choose to be obedient to the Word of God. I crucify the flesh. The flesh is dead." (Author's paraphrase)

As you now go into the store, you are going in the power of the Holy Spirit, infused with inner strength. You go in as a conqueror, not a coward. You are in charge of the situation, not a victim of it. You are really experiencing *living free*.

> *"But now we are discharged from the Law and have terminated all intercourse with it, having died to what once restrained and held us captive. So now we serve not under [obedience to] the old code of written regulations, but [under obedience to the promptings] of the Spirit in newness [of life]." Romans 7:6*

God is saying to me:

Thoughts I'm having today:

I've shared with the Lord:

Further thoughts and prayers:

Dying to the Flesh

Romans 8:12, 13

Romans, chapter 8, verses 12 through 13, says: ". . . we are debtors, not to the flesh, to live after the flesh. For if ye live after the flesh, ye shall die; but if ye through the spirit do mortify the deeds of the body, ye shall live." (KJV)

I don't want to die. I want to live. I want life to be full and complete with fulfillment and purpose. How about you?

Scripture is clear and precise in its promise of a full life. But the flesh has to die. We cannot live a life devoted to the demands of the flesh and expect to have the abundant life that Christ has promised us.

Think of your life right now. Would you have to say you are living a life devoted to the flesh or to the Spirit? What about yesterday? How many times did you insist upon and get your own way about something? Even more specific—how many times did you eat what you wanted even though your body didn't need what you ate? Perhaps you ate something that you didn't even want, or even like! These actions are the result of a life given over to the demands of the flesh (and in some cases, just plain lazy habits).

But there *is* hope! The Scriptures contain plain instructions for how to stop living a life devoted to the flesh and begin living a life devoted to the things of God. The Bible tells us to *mortify* the deeds of the body.

To mortify means to discipline one's body and appetites through self-denial. In other words, *do without.* Say "no" to yourself. Cut down. Go on a fast—if you feel the Lord is prompting you to that.

Reinforce your decision to mortify the deeds of the body by telling yourself the truth from God's Word:

"I am a debtor, but not to the flesh. I am not obligated to my carnal nature—to live a life ruled by the standards set up by the dictates of the flesh—because if I live by the dictates of the flesh, I will surely die. But if by the power of the Holy

Spirit I am habitually putting to death the deeds prompted by the body, I will really live forever." (Author's paraphrase)

In the area of overeating, it may mean facing a tempting food item and saying, "I don't *have* to eat that." "I don't *need* to buy this."

In the area of overspending, you can deny self by offering God your checkbook, and asking Him where to give your money instead of spending it on something you want but really don't need.

Develop the habit of consulting God first before eating or spending something extra. We are not free, as His servants, to eat what we want, or spend what we want, but to seek His direction.

Doing God's will in all the details of our lives is really *living free.*

"So, then, brethren, we are debtors, but not to the flesh—we are not obligated to our carnal nature—to live [a life ruled by the standards set up by the dictates] of the flesh. For if you live according to [the dictates of] the flesh you will surely die. But if through the power of the (Holy) Spirit you are habitually putting to death—making extinct, deadening—the [evil] deeds prompted by the body, you shall (really and genuinely) live forever." Romans 8:12, 13

God is saying to me:

Thoughts I'm having today:

I've shared with the Lord:

Further thoughts and prayers:

Exercise

Romans 8:18

"Exercise? Who, me? You've got to be kidding!" I strained at the thought of it. How much more does God want of me anyway? Isn't He going to leave any area of my life alone? You know the answer.

1 Corinthians, chapter 9, verses 24-27, says: "Do you not know that in a race all the runners run, but only one gets the prize? Run in such a way as to get the prize. Everyone who competes in the games goes into strict training. They do it to get a crown that will not last, but we do it to get a crown that will last forever. Therefore I do not run like a man running aimlessly, I do not fight like a man beating the air. No, I beat my body and make it my slave so that after I have preached to others, I myself will not be disqualified for the prize." (NIV)

Who says exercise has to be hard and dull, leaving me weak and out of breath? I have found that I can be gentle with my body, quietly bringing it into submission with love, care and diligence. For instance, I can take it for a bike ride in the fresh air or run just for fun, and enjoy every moment. I can walk in the park or swing on the swing. Daily giving my body a break from housework or office work and other things that tax its strength can be relaxing and refreshing.

Exercise is also bringing my body under submission to the Word of God. I am not my body's slave; I am its master. I don't have to beat it to death. But I can gently coax and encourage my body into the discipline of exercise. I feed on the Word of God, eat good, healthy foods, and allow my body some physical exertion through exercise. Think of the glory of being disciplined and renewed by our heavenly Father, and you can do just a couple more sit-ups, run a little more, swim a little longer, bike a little farther. Exercise is truly a part of *living free.*

"[But what of that?] For I consider that the sufferings

of this present time (this present life) are not worth be-ing compared with the glory that is about to be re-vealed to us and in us and for us, and conferred on us!
Romans 8:18

God is saying to me:

Thoughts I'm having today:

I've shared with the Lord:

Further thoughts and prayers:

More Than Conquerors

Romans 8:35-37

A lady in Canada once told me: "Although I have been a committed Christian for almost ten years, I have been a slave to my appetite for the past three years. It seems that no amount of prayer or self-effort has helped." Sound familiar?

One thing that I have learned as a Christian in the last few years is that we are not exempt from the fight, but we are empowered for it. We are not going to have it easy all the time, but we can be prepared to face the problems we have with the Word of God.

Scripture points out very clearly that we have authority over the devil, but that we are to subdue the flesh. In fact, the Bible calls it warfare—the flesh against the spirit, and vice versa. Know this, that we can be free from the flesh, we can die to what once held us captive.

Defeat can be defined as the result of a battle lost or a problem unsolved. For us to say that we will never, never be defeated is to fool ourselves and be unprepared. But defeat is not the end of all things. It can serve us to learn how to deal with it and overcome.

Let's look into the Word of God: In Romans, chapter 8, verses 35-37, we read that nothing can separate us from the love of Jesus—not suffering, affliction, or tribulation. Calamity cannot, nor distress. Persecution cannot separate us from His love, neither hunger nor destitution, peril or sword. Rather, through these things in our lives, we experience death for Christ's sake all day long. We may be ready to say that we believe that nothing can separate us from God's love, but are we willing to actually experience some trials and prove it?

Listen to the most powerful part of this passage: It says that amid all these things we are more than conquerors—not apart from, but amid. Not in the absence of suffering, but in the face of it. We are not exempt from tribulation, but triumphant through it.

When God helps me to watch carefully what I eat, in order to lose weight, it does not mean that I will never be hungry, but that I can be hungry and still not eat. It means that even on those days when my flesh cries out to consume large quantities of food, I am more than a conqueror. Even amid times of defeat, I am still more than a conqueror, through Him. Defeat can teach us many things. Satan intends defeat to overwhelm us: "You're finished." But we can turn the tables on him. A victorious person is one who conquers even defeat and learns something positive from it. Pick yourself up from defeat and go on. Amid all the things you face in your life today, you are a conqueror, you are *living free*.

> *"Who shall ever separate us from Christ's love? Shall suffering and affliction and tribulation? Or calamity and distress? Or persecution, or hunger, or destitution, or peril, or sword? Even as it is written, for Thy sake we are put to death all the day long, we are regarded and counted as sheep for the slaughter [Ps. 44:22]. Yet amid all these things we are more than conquerors and gain a surpassing victory through Him Who loved us."*
> Romans 8:35-37

God is saying to me:

Thoughts I'm having today:

I've shared with the Lord:

Further thoughts and prayers:

God's Love

Romans 8:38, 39

I received a letter from a lady in Rio de Janeiro, Brazil. She says: "About a year ago, I began to pray to God to liberate me from my weight problem. And I began to lose weight. I lost a lot and I know that the Lord blessed me in this. But the problem of food continues. I still have an anxious struggle over a good dish. I know that this is a weakness to the point of a lack of faith; however, it is totally involuntary. I still like to eat!

"I believe in Jesus and I know that He can liberate me and heal every area of weakness in my life. It is because of this that I believe God can give me some answers through your experience in this area.

"I am not looking for a new method to reduce. I am not wishing to lose weight in order to be 'prettier.' What I am looking for is to be liberated from something that has hindered Jesus from being seen in me.

"I need to be freed from the desire to eat. It is as though there is a curtain that clouds the vision of the things of Jesus. But I have faith that this veil will soon be lifted. I know that He is interested in everything that concerns our lives. Will you help me?"

I think this letter is a beautiful example of a searching heart—a heart perfect before God, even though habits and behaviors are not perfect. As children of God, we have beautiful assurance from the Bible that nothing can ever separate us from Him. If something comes between us and God, it is of our own doing; He has promised that His love remains the same.

What are some things that have crept into your life today so that you feel you cannot experience the love of God fully? Hold onto the scripture for today. It is for you. Apply it to your present situation, paraphrase it to include the things that you face today. For example: "I am persuadeed that neither death, nor life, nor angels, nor principalities, nor things impending, nor food binges, nor guilt, nor self-condemnation, nor my own failure, nor Hershey bars, nor Snickers, nor Coke, nor pie, nor anything else in all creation will be able to separate me from the love of God which is in Christ Jesus."

To learn to walk in the wonder of God's love with no separation is really *living free*.

"For I am persuaded beyond doubt—am sure—that neither death, nor life, nor angels, nor principalities, nor things impending and threatening, nor things to come, nor powers, nor height, nor depth, nor anything else in all creation will be able to separate us from the love of God which is in Christ Jesus our Lord." Romans 8:38, 39

God is saying to me:

Thoughts I'm having today:

I've shared with the Lord:

Further thoughts and prayers:

God's Mercy

Romans 9:15, 16

I try and I try and still I fail. I make all kinds of resolutions and declarations in the early hours of the day and by noon I have eaten everything I can lay my hands on. I will never make it. I will always be fat. Did you ever feel like that? I have many times.

One day, when I was feeling especially low and defeated, my Bible fell open to Romans chapter 9, verses 15 and 16: "I will have mercy on whom I have mercy, and I will have compassion on whom I have compassion. It does not, therefore, depend on man's desire or effort, but on God's mercy."

First of all, we must remind ourselves again that it is only in complete surrender and dependence upon God that we will come into any measure of success. We can't desire enough or strain hard enough to make ourselves lose weight, or stop smoking, or have pure thoughts. But we can place ourselves totally upon God's mercy.

Our determination sometimes wanes, but God's mercy endures forever. Our desires vascilate, but God's mercy remains the same. Our efforts may prove to be futile, but God's mercy is everlasting. We may fail at times, but God's mercy is unfailing. We may be saturated with guilt, but God in His mercy desires to forgive us and to cleanse us from guilt through His precious blood.

Our success is not dependent upon us, but upon our dependence upon God. When we get discouraged and want to give up, we must remind ourselves that God never gives up. Instead of focusing on our shortcomings, we need to get into God's Word and focus on Him. Don't dwell in defeat, live in the Word of God.

When you feel as though you will never make it, and defeat seems imminent, receive the words of Romans 9:15-16. God's gift does not depend on your own human will or effort, but on God's mercy. Continuing to live according to the Word of God is essential to *living free.*

> *"For He says to Moses, I will have mercy on whom I will have mercy and I will have compassion (pity) on whom I will have compassion [Exod. 33:19]. So then [God's gift] is not a question of human will and human effort, but of God's mercy. It depends not on one's own willingness nor on his strenuous exertion as in running a race, but on God's having mercy on him." Romans 9:15, 16*

God is saying to me:

Thoughts I'm having today:

I've shared with the Lord:

Further thoughts and prayers:

Ephesians Encouragements

Do you ever feel worn out and defeated? Are you ever tempted to just give up and resign from the human race? Does that daily walk seem to tire you more and more? Are you just plain weary of trying to be a good Christian? Are you tempted to throw in the towel and just remain average—or less? Then I have news for you.

I have found that the book of Ephesians contains wonderful encouragement. The words are just for you! Now, don't you feel encouraged already?

The Word of God is mighty, and it was written for you. Yes, YOU. . . . It doesn't matter how you feel right now. God's Word remains the same. God's Word is the only truth you can actually count on. Go ahead, pick it up and read it, personalize it, live it. You will find that your life will change. Take encouragement from Ephesians 1:3: "Praise be to the God and Father of our Lord Jesus Christ, who has blessed us in the heavenly realms with every spiritual blessing in Christ." In my own life I paraphrase that verse, putting it into the first person and pray it back to God. I say: "I give blessing and praise to you, Father, and the Father of my Savior. You have blessed me with every spiritual blessing in Christ Jesus."

This is the first step I take toward a more positive outlook on my life and the day ahead of me. How many times do we wait to give praise to God until the day seems bright? Should we wait until the circumstances are right and everything seems to be going our way before we give praise and blessing to God? The order should be reversed. To face the hard situations of life, to be strong enough to confront any circumstance in a positive manner, we must first be in the habit of praising and blessing God.

The Scriptures tell us that we are already blessed with every spiritual blessing in Christ Jesus, no matter how it looks at the moment. God's Word is true. Won't you stop today and give praise to God, blessing the name of the Lord? Your outlook will be so transformed that whatever you face today you will be able to handle. You will be moving in the power of God's Word. You will be *living free.*

I Am Somebody

Ephesians 1:4

Do you ever feel as though you are invisible? Do you seem to melt into the mass of people in the shopping center? Are you just a number at the bank? Do people regard you, like the I.R.S., as a Social Security number with taxes due?

I have these feelings some days. You could see me walking down the street, and not necessarily notice me. I am just an average person, another face in the crowd. I wonder if people even realize that I have feelings at all. The bag boy at the supermarket shoves my grocery-laden cart at me without a hint of willingness to help me put the groceries in the car; the bank teller sends my paperwork back to me through the drive-in window with an electronic "thank you." I am even a middle child! When I was growing up I was either too young or too old for most things.

I recently moved from another state. The state I came from doesn't consider me a resident anymore, and the state I have moved to says I haven't been here long enough to be counted as a resident. I guess that makes me a nonresident!

Attending a new church, I see the same people week after week, but I have had to repeat my name two or three times each Sunday. It wouldn't be so bad, except that everyone thinks I should already know *their* names!

I get letters from ministries around the country who have had my name put into a computer, and the label prints out in little impersonal dots instead of typewritten letters.

But, you know, it really doesn't matter. . . . I *am* somebody, and God knows who I am! He planned my life before I was born! Read Psalm 139. I am His, and I am precious to Him.

Let the grocery boy treat me with indifference; God treats me personally as His own child. Let the computer spit out my name in little dots; God wrote my name in the Lamb's Book of Life.

The whole world can ignore me and treat me as if I weren't

there at all, but God has picked me out to be His very own.

The next time you see me walking down the street, whistling a little tune, know this, I have probably just remembered who I am, and especially who I am to God.

I am His. I belong. I am somebody special. And so are you!

Ephesians 1:4 tells me that God picked me out to be His own long before the world was created. He planned that I would be His alone, blameless before Him in Jesus. Thank you, Father. In you, I have discovered what *living free* means.

"Even as [in His love] He chose us—actually picked us out for Himself as His own—in Christ before the foundation of the world; that we should be holy (consecrated and set apart for Him) and blameless in His sight, even above reproach, before Him in love." Ephesians 1:4

God is saying to me:

Thoughts I'm having today:

I've shared with the Lord:

Further thoughts and prayers:

Redeemed

Ephesians 1:7, 8

Have you ever thought about what it means to be redeemed?

I remember, as a new bride, shopping at stores that gave trading stamps with every purchase. I collected them diligently and each week I pasted them neatly into the book.

During the months of accumulating these stamps, I would look through the catalog and dream about what I would trade them for. First, I would select something very practical, then I would decide on some luxury item that I wouldn't ordinarily buy. I changed my mind fifty times.

Finally, when I had four or five books of trading stamps, off to the redemption center I would go, and come home with something entirely different than I had planned!

Items I secured at a redemption center were not purchased there; they were redeemed. They were actually paid for at the supermarket or the gas station, but I didn't come into full possession of the new mixer or lamp until I picked it up at the center. After I had "redeemed" my selection, it was mine to use as I wished.

This is a simple example of what it means to be redeemed by the Lord. First, He bought us, and then He claimed us.

Ephesians 1:7 says I have redemption through His blood. I was bought and paid for at the cross. But I need to claim that salvation and its full benefits to make it my own. Then Jesus has full right to my life and can use me in His service as He sees fit. It doesn't matter what I have done or been in the past, for the Bible tells me that I have not only redemption but remission of all my offenses—all covered by the blood of Jesus at the cross.

I also have access to the riches of His favor, a right to be in the presence of the living God. He redeemed me and now He desires to use me.

"In Him we have redemption (deliverance and salva-

43

tion) through His blood, the remission (forgiveness) of our offenses (shortcomings and trespasses), in accordance with the riches and the generosity of His gracious favor, which He lavished upon us in every kind of wisdom and understanding (practical insight and prudence). Ephesians 1: 7, 8.

God is saying to me:

Thoughts I'm having today:

I've shared with the Lord:

Further thoughts and prayers:

Help

Ephesians 2:5, 6

There are times when I can sense the presence of God and easily accept His help. Then there are days when I actually hesitate to go to the Lord.

Does this ever happen to you?

Why do we hesitate to go to the Lord for help? The letters I get from many reveal that God's people find it easier to pray when they are on top of things than when they are down or experiencing defeat.

There is nothing in the Scriptures that indicates that God loves us any less when we are not doing as well as we could, or that He loves us any more when we do well. The Scriptures tell us that God loves us—period.

I had a weight problem I struggled with for years. I prayed about everything else. I asked the Lord to give me direction, strength over temptation, wisdom and knowledge in every area—except this one. I never wanted to talk about my problem with anyone, including God!

Finally, the day came when I felt so desperate and guilty about overeating that I went before the Lord and poured out my heart. I confessed my weaknesses, independence, willfulness and stubbornness to Him. I asked Jesus to help me in this area just as He had in other areas of my life. I knew He loved me as I was, overweight or not, and I knew that I was a Christian in spite of my weight. Knowing is what gave me courage to face Him at last.

This is the verse that came alive for me at that time. It is from Ephesians, chapter two, paraphrased into my own words with an eye on my own problems: "Even when I was dead in my sins and shortcomings, God through Jesus raised me up to be alive and in fellowship with Christ. I don't deserve this, but it's true. In Jesus, through the grace of God, I have now been raised and sit together with Him in the heavenly sphere."

To wait until I am temporarily free of the circumstance or

problem to talk to God about it is foolish—there is no help for me apart from Christ. Every other solution has proved to be only temporary relief, not lasting victory. I didn't have to hide my shortcomings, only acknowledge them to a gracious and loving Father who understood me and knew my needs before I asked for help.

Whatever your problem is today, though it may not be the same as mine, is answered in God, through Jesus. Won't you let Him help you today? Confide in Him. He made a provision to help you—it is Jesus himself.

A loving heavenly Father and a personal Savior provide the way for *living free.*

"Even when we were dead [slain] by [our own] short-comings and trespasses, He made us alive together in fellowship and in union with Christ.—He gave us the very life of Christ Himself, the same new life with which He quickened Him. [For] it is by grace—by His favor and mercy which you did not deserve—that you are saved (delivered from judgment and made partakers of Christ's salvation). And He raised us up together with Him and made us sit down together—giving us joint seating with Him—in the heavenly sphere [by virtue of our being] in Christ Jesus, the Messiah, the Anointed One." Ephesians 2:5, 6

God is saying to me:

Thoughts I'm having today:

I've shared with the Lord:

Further thoughts and prayers:

His Handiwork

Ephesians 2:10

While flying over the United States on my way to teach seminars or to keep a speaking engagement, I have marveled at the face of the earth neatly divided up into squares of alfalfa green, wheat amber and dark brown. It is like a great quilt. Fences provide the stitching, and roads the borders. The seams run east and west, north and south. I know that man didn't intend to create the quilt effect, but through his handiwork and labor he has done just that.

My grandmother has made a number of quilts, cutting first the squares, then stitching, backing and filling them to cover her family with the colorful masterpieces. Her handiwork is appreciated and admired by all the aunts and cousins. Her handiwork has had much the same effect on me as the sight of the farmland from the air.

My mother crocheted an afghan and my aunts used to crochet lace doilies. Each started out with just a ball of string, a hook, and a pattern or an idea to create their piece of art. Others I have known have excelled in cooking, sewing or painting. I have a friend who has a tremendous talent for homemaking and hostessing. Others have talent as Bible study teachers, feeding new Christians, and making disciples.

Ephesians, chapter two, tells me that I am God's own handiwork. His specialty is creating me—making me and molding me into the image of His Son, Jesus. And because I am His own handiwork, I am equipped to do those things that He has for me to do. I am not free to be *anything* I want to be, rather released to be the full person *He* wants me to be—not to live up to my full potential, but His. It is now up to me to determine His will among all the choices I face. Since I am God's own special project, what projects do I pursue?—only the ones He gives me peace in pursuing. Otherwise, my life would be cluttered with nonessentials.

God did not save me so that I could now do something *for*

Him. He saved me so He could live and work through me. Now because I am His child, He enables me to do only those things He has called me to do.

Remembering this scripture has helped me to take a closer look at the projects that clamor to be done. Finding out the direction God has for me had to come first. Once I knew that, I began to see which things should take priority. I don't sing in the choir simply because the choir needs voices, but because it is an expression of worship that God has given me. Think about it, Sunday school teacher, church worker, teacher. When we do those things God has called us to do, we are enabled for the task.

I am God's own handiwork. He is working in me as a farmer works in the field—preparing the ground, sowing seed, reaping the harvest, and starting over again. He has a work for me to do, that's true, but He also has a work to do in me. Letting God work in me and doing what He has called me to do is really *living free.*

"For we are God's [own] handiwork (His workmanship), recreated in Christ Jesus, [born anew] that we may do those good works which God predestined (planned beforehand) for us, (taking paths which He prepared ahead of time) that we should walk in them—living the good life which He prearranged and made ready for us to live." Ephesians 2:10

God is saying to me:

Thoughts I'm having today:

I've shared with the Lord:

Further thoughts and prayers:

Included

Ephesians 2:19

Do you ever feel as though the world is passing you by? Do you ever feel like an outsider?

I have a young cousin who recently came to know Jesus as her personal Savior. She and her husband watched as one by one their friends dropped them. "We were no longer accepted in the group," she told me.

Excluded. What an empty feeling.

Family members may have social gatherings leaving out the Christian members. Neighbors sometimes group in someone else's backyard and you discover that you have not been invited. Left out. Excluded. Even though you know that some of the activities or the conversation is not what you would want to participate in, there is still that emptiness, that hollow feeling.

Let's focus on the opportunity of being included in the family of God.

Ephesians, chapter two tells us about this wonderful miracle. In times when the world seems to leave us out, we need to remind ourselves that the reverse is true. I am no longer an outsider, excluded and devoid of the rights of citizenship. I share citizenship with the saints. . . . I am of God's own people, consecrated and set apart for God himself. . . . I belong to God's own household. Yes, when the commitment of your heart is secure in the Word of God, those who are not serving the Lord will begin to feel uncomfortable with you around.

You carry the presence of God within you. Jesus was despised and rejected of men. This is an opportunity to identify with Him. Shake off the temptation to feel sorry for yourself, and rejoice instead in the fact that you are included in the family of God.

Love those who would leave you out, go out of your way to be kind and hospitable to them. But remember, God's people do not need to be included in the ways of the world to be happy and feel secure. Our security is in Him and in the family of God.

Cultivate relationships among people in the family of God, and pray for the family to be extended even more through your witness to those who would exclude you. Being free from the world, making friends in God's family, sharing citizenship with the saints, not the world, this is *living free*.

> *"Therefore you are no longer outsiders—exiles, migrants and aliens, excluded from the rights of citizens; but you now share citizenship with the saints—God's own people, consecrated and set apart for Himself; and you belong to God's [own] household." Ephesians 2:19*

God is saying to me:

Thoughts I'm having today:

I've shared with the Lord:

Further thoughts and prayers:

Access to the Father

Ephesians 3:12

We receive several letters each month which say something like this: "I have read your book," or "I heard you speak, and am so happy for the miracle God has done in your life. Now that God has helped you, do you think that you could help me?"

The answer is no. I can't help you. At least, not in the way you think. I can only show you the Lord, and the verses He has helped me with from the Bible.

What people imply through their inquiries is that only I can learn and receive from God, and they in turn must receive from me. One of the greatest pleasures of my whole ministry is teaching Christians how to have a quiet time with the Lord and to hear Him speak directly to them!

You may not feel as though you have the right to hear from God directly. You may feel inferior, unworthy, or guilty. But it is not because of what I have done or what I am that I hear from God. Rather, it is because of what He has done and who He is that I can hear from Him. And so can you. All we have to do is to put our faith and trust in Jesus and we have free access.

To be bold and daring in ourselves would be to come into the presence of God with arrogance, but when we come into His presence because of Jesus, it is our right—He gave us that right. When we stand in Jesus, we have the courage to face our God, we have the confidence to know that when we approach Him in the name of Jesus, He will never send us away or make us wait in line or have an appointment. We will always be welcomed by our Father. Not because of who we are, but because of who He is.

I have an unhindered approach to God, with freedom and without fear. I don't have to clean up my act to come to God; I come to God and He helps me clean up my act. I don't beg my way into His presence, I present myself in confidence, because of Jesus' sacrifice for me.

What is on your heart today? Don't try to straighten it all out and have your plan of action ready to submit for approval. Go to the Father and listen to His plan and then obey. Tell Him the problem and then wait for the solution. You can only see your side; He can see all sides. Stand on the Word of God and present yourself in the throne room. You will find your Father has been waiting to talk with you. He loves you; He gives you free access; He helps you to *live free.*

"In Whom, because of our faith in Him, we dare to have the boldness (courage and confidence) of free access— an unreserved approach to God with freedom and without fear." Ephesians 3:12

God is saying to me:

Thoughts I'm having today:

I've shared with the Lord:

Further thoughts and prayers:

Strength

Ephesians 3:16

"If I weren't so weak, I could stop. . . ."

"The temptation is just so great I can't resist. . . ."

"I know I shouldn't, but if you insist. . . ."

"Well, I am on a diet, but since you made it just for me, I guess I'll have just one." Sound familiar?

I remember one Christmas season doing all my shopping without eating in the department stores. What a victory! I also attended a reception without having a piece of the wedding cake! There was a little pressure from a few of the other guests, but you know the couple was still married even though I didn't have any of their cake!

It has not always been like this. There were days when I couldn't go into a shopping center without having a little snack—usually candy that I could just fit into my purse and no one would even notice. And there are countless weddings in my past where I not only ate my piece of wedding cake, but occasionally finished up whatever my children left on their plates as well.

There came a day when the words of Ephesians, chapter 3, verse 16, came to life for me. Look at this passage of scripture paraphrased into the first person: "Out of the rich treasury of His glory, I am strengthened and reinforced with mighty power in my inner self because the Holy Spirit of God himself indwells my innermost being and personality."

Think of it; I am not weak, I am strong. Reinforced with the mighty power of God. Not a patched-up job on the outside, but from the inside—my inner self is reinforced. God doesn't just leave me to my whims, but gets inside me to my deep desires. Another miracle is that God doesn't send someone else to fix me up and strengthen me, but it is the Holy Spirit of God himself who indwells my innermost being and personality.

Isn't it wonderful to know that God does not expect us to

be strong on our own, but reaches into our innermost being and provides the strength we need?

You are strong today if you know the Lord. God is not short on strength. It is out of the rich treasury of His glory that He gives us the strength we need.

What are you facing today? Remember that you are not weak; you are strong in the Lord because the Lord is strong in you. Meditate on being infused with strength from the inside out. You are brave and courageous, strong and mighty because the Almighty God indwells you. This is a day in which you can depend on the Lord to give you strength from the inside out to *live free.*

"May He grant you out of the rich treasury of His glory to be strengthened and reinforced with mighty power in the inner man by the (Holy) Spirit [Himself]— indwelling your innermost being and personality." Ephesians 3:16.

God is saying to me:

Thoughts I'm having today:

I've shared with the Lord:

Further thoughts and prayers:

The Love of God

Ephesians 3:18

When I was a little girl I knew a song that went like this, "Nobody loves me, everybody hates me, I'm gonna go eat worms. . . ." I used to think about those words and wonder what would happen if I really did eat worms. Would eating worms suddenly, by magic, transform me into a more lovable person? Or would it make me so sick that everyone would immediately be concerned and lovingly hover over me until I was well again? Or would I die, and everyone would be sorry for not treating me with the love I thought I deserved?

Childish thoughts—but I have met adults that are convinced that they are truly unloved and unlovable. They do and say thoughtless and hateful things. They look unlovable by taking on sour expressions—in a way they're eating worms. I have counseled with people who have claimed that because they did not have a good home life or a good relationship with their earthly father, a love relationship with God is impossible for them. But that's not true. It might make it a little harder, but with God nothing is impossible.

Ephesians, chapter 3, verse 18, tells us that we have the power and strength to apprehend and grasp the experience of God's love because Christ, through our faith, actually dwells, settles down, and makes His permanent home in our hearts. God gives us His love through Jesus, but we have to grasp it. He extends to us His love, but we must receive it. You may feel unloved, but that doesn't make it true. You may feel unlovable, but you are not.

When God dwells in us He supplies us with a reservoir of love. He intends that the reservoir be full to overflowing, turning into a river that flows out and touches others.

He loves you today. I would repeat it eighty times if it would help to reach your spirit today. He loves you and will be as close to you as you will allow Him. He expresses His love to you each day through His Word, with verses like this one:

61

" . . . with the harmony of the universe providing a stable place to live where we can be sure that morning follows the dark night."

Don't say you can't experience God's love. Receive the truth of this passage of scripture into your spirit. You have the power and strength to apprehend and grasp the experience of God's love because of Jesus, who through your faith actually dwells, settles down, and makes His permanent home in your heart.

You don't have to stretch to reach God, only open up to embrace Him. Experience His love, discover the depth of it; you are free to grasp the love of God because you are *living free.*

"That you may have the power and be strong to appre-hend and grasp with all the saints (God's devoted peo-ple, the experience of that love) what is the breadth and length and height and depth [of it]." Ephesians 3:18

God is saying to me:

Thoughts I'm having today:

I've shared with the Lord:

Further thoughts and prayers:

God at Work in Me

Ephesians 3:20

It is God that is at work in me—I must remember that. He is performing that which concerns me and that which concerns Him. No matter how I fare, at best I am only cooperating with Him—He is doing the work.

I am unable to carry out the will of God except He works in me. He is able to carry out His purpose in me far better than I can. When I *try* to be what God wants me to be, I am doomed to disappointment. But when I allow Him to enable and empower me, I find His purpose being carried out far beyond my wildest dreams and hopes.

I spend time dreaming and thinking about what I would like to accomplish, and what I would like to be, and then when I have reached the limits of what I could possibly dream of accomplishing, I just take a moment to remember and consider that God can do far more than that.

He can make me a person worthy of the love of others, and even of myself. He can make me strong and stable in the face of temptation and defeat. He can free me from bondage. He enlightens me and makes me wise instead of confused and foolish. He gives me joy and laughter instead of depression and crying, peace and rest in place of fear and struggle.

It is God who is at work in me. Can't you tell? How else would I be making such progress? How else could I grow toward the express image of His Son? It is God who is at work in me.

I must remember that it is not by my own efforts that His work is being accomplished in me and is responsible for my changed attitudes and outlook. He is accomplishing His will in my heart and life. It is His work within me that enables me to change my habits; it is His working within me that is changing me as a person. I am being remolded into a usable vessel by His loving hands. If I should try with all my might and fail, no matter, it is only the changes He's making and the work He is doing in me that will really make a difference.

When we think about our scripture for today, and the magnificent wonder of the Almighty God working in the lives of His children, we can pick up and go on. We can walk free from failure, free from condemnation of our shortcomings. It is God who is at work in us. He is able to carry out His purposes in us and He can do superabundantly over and above all that we dare ask or think. It is true that we are not able, but He is.

Go ahead—ask; dare to dream. What do you need today? God can do it; in fact He can do more than you ask—more than you dream. When God is at work in you, you are *living free*.

> *"Now to Him Who, by (in consequence of) the [action of His] power that is at work within us, is able to [carry out His purpose and] do superabundantly, far over and above all that we dare ask or think—infinitely beyond our highest prayers, desires, thoughts, hopes or dreams." Ephesians 3:20*

God is saying to me:

Thoughts I'm having today:

I've shared with the Lord:

Further thoughts and prayers:

Philippian Friends

A friend is defined as "one attached to another by esteem and affection; an intimate associate." Jesus wants to be that kind of friend to you. He left us His Word to be the verbal confirmation of that relationship. A friend is one who will tell us the truth. The Scripture will prove to be truth in the face of deceptive circumstances; it will always tell the truth even when we are lying to ourselves about our sin, our person, or our worth.

Dig now into Philippians with me and discover the friendliness of the Truth. Apply it to your life. Stop telling yourself you can't make it when the truth is that you can. Stop telling yourself you don't have anyone when Philippians tells you that Jesus has "laid hold of me, and made me His own." Don't say that God has given up on you. Philippians says that He began a good work, that it is a good work and that He won't quit. Don't say you don't have any friends; you have these "Philippian Friends," and you have Jesus.

A Good Work

Philippians 1:6

Today you face another day. But do you face it as the same person you were yesterday? Are you aware that God is working in you each and every day? Are you cooperating with Him in this work or do you resist?

Philippians, chapter 1, verse 6, tells us this: "He began a good work; He will complete it." What work is He doing? When did He begin it and when will it end?

Galatians, chapter 5, verses 22 and 23, tells us about the work going on inside each of us who are filled with the Holy Spirit. The Amplified Bible says it this way: "The work which His presence within us accomplishes." This work includes love, peace, patience, kindness, goodness, faithfulness, gentleness and self-control. We must remember that these attributes (works) are not instantaneous but develop and grow. The Bible calls them fruit. Fruit starts growing from a little blossom.

Here in Southern California, there are some citrus trees that have both full ripe fruit on them and blossoms at the same time. It is like that with us. In some areas we may be mature and developed and in other areas just a little bud. Some may display great love for others but very little patience toward everyday annoyances. Some are very kind, and outgoing, meeting the needs of others, but lack in self-control. Remember the full fruit and blossoms are at the same time, on the same tree. We are ever-bearing, fruit-producing beings.

But, it seems to take so long. The fruit is so slow in coming to maturity. Remember, the words of Philippians, chapter 1, verse 6: "The work fully accomplished will go on until Jesus comes." It is a lifelong thing. There will always be fruit in the development stage. I will always be producing a crop and promising a crop at the same time. This is not an instantaneous miracle, but again, a fruit, produced in its season. Throughout the time allotted to me on this earth, I will have fruit coming to maturity. According to Scripture, God is in no hurry. He prunes, waters, cultivates and cares. He began the work, He will bring it to completion, not by working on me, but in me.

Today look to the Holy Spirit, drawing strength to allow Him to finish what He began. Don't give up on God; He isn't giving up on you. The fruit is growing—remember the fragrance of the orange blossoms? The blossoms bring pleasantness too. Enjoy the growth process. You will make it—a tree planted by the water, growing, *living free.*

"And I am convinced and sure of this very thing, that He who began a good work in you will continue until the day of Jesus Christ—right up to the time of His return—developing [that good work] and perfecting and bringing it to full completion in you." Philippians 1:6

God is saying to me:

Thoughts I'm having today:

I've shared with the Lord:

Further thoughts and prayers:

Not Ashamed

Philippians 1:20

I recently attended a large convention where there were many receptions and food everywhere. Long days spent in visiting with people and walking around the large convention center absorbing new ideas makes one really hungry! How was I to handle the parties and ALL THAT FOOD?

I have a very true friend in Philippians, chapter 1, verse 20. I called upon my friend for the reinforcement I needed. Listen to the words that helped me so much. The New International Version says: "I eagerly expect and hope that I will in no way be ashamed, but will have sufficient courage so that now as always Christ will be exalted in my body, whether by life or by death."

"I will in no way be ashamed." I knew that as I stood on the Word of God I could attend the receptions, eat moderately and make wise choices. I knew that while my heart was right before God, He would protect me. I counted on Him to see to it that there was food that I could eat.

And there it was—fruit, cheese, and crackers. Not just one kind of fruit, but a variety; not just some cheese, but little cuts of every kind. A wonderful banquet spread for ME, which allowed me to use good judgement, and have an opportunity to prove God's Word. I was not ashamed. I was not disgraced by the foods that I ate. I could talk to anyone, allowing them to see what was on my plate, without shame. I was in control. It was wonderful.

What do you face today? A situation that before has proven to be your undoing? It may not be a matter of food for you. Perhaps you have said something you now regret. Claim this friend from Philippians, chapter one. Maybe your relationship with a teenage child is not what you would like; conversations turn into arguments instead of calm discussion, and later you are ashamed of your words or reactions. Claim this verse.

Here it is paraphrased and amplified: "I shall not disgrace myself nor be put to shame in anything: but with the utmost freedom of speech and unfailing courage, now as always, Christ the Messiah will be magnified and get glory and praise in this body of mine and be boldly exalted in my person."

No shame. No disgrace. Freedom, courage, glorifying Jesus in my behavior, in my conversation, in my choices. I do not have to be afraid. I am free. I exhalt the person of Jesus. I am capable of living a life free of embarrassment and disgrace. Because of Jesus, I live above the negative, I live in the positive; I am *living free.*

"This is in keeping with my own eager desire and persistent expectation and hope, that I shall not disgrace myself nor be put to shame in anything; but that with the utmost freedom of speech and unfailing courage, now as always heretofore, Christ, the Messiah, will be magnified and get glory and praise in this body of mine and be boldly exalted in my person, whether through (by) life or through (by) death." Philippians 1:20

God is saying to me:

Thoughts I'm having today:

I've shared with the Lord:

Further thoughts and prayers:

Christ-life

Philippians 1:21

Why am I here? Why do I even exist? Did you ever ask these questions? Do you know for sure why you are here on this earth?

Philippians, chapter 1, verse 21, gives the Christian the answer to this most perplexing question. We live, or exist, or have our being in Christ. That is why this is the meaning of life for the Christian. We actually live out the life of Christ. He is not dead. He is, in fact, seated at the right hand of the Father, but He also by the power of the Holy Spirit, lives in us. When we accept Jesus as our Savior, He then resides or lives in us and lives out His life through ours.

This is the basis for our philosophical position as Christians. We live in and for Him. He gives our life meaning. No one else, or nothing else can do that. Christ gives my life a foundation—a basis for existence. He affects my opinions, my views, my values. It is a new life perspective for me. To live is Christ.

How about you? How is your commitment today? Does your life have meaning and purpose?

It is so easy for the young mother to feel that her accomplishments in life are wiping little noses and mopping up floors. As the children grow older, she thinks of herself as the cookie-baker or the taxi-driver. But when her life is based in Jesus, when she lives and moves in Him, she realizes her responsibilities in a far different light. She knows how important it is to wipe those little noses and floors with love, ministering to the needs of others. It can be a very satisfying job. She does not feel trapped; she senses purpose in the activities of the day.

For me, to live in Christ means that everything I do, I do in His name. To live means the opposite of dying. We don't need to feel removed from the realities of life. We can really have an extraordinary sense of purpose in whatever we do. For us to live is Christ—we let His life flow out through us.

We can reach a level of patience with others that the natural man finds impossible. Why? Because it is Christ's life flowing through us. We accomplish the impossible because it is Christ in us. We become what to others is only a dream because we dare to believe in God's Word and let His Word tell us what to do; we aren't limited by our own resources.

For me to live is Christ. What would Christ do in this situation? What would Christ say to that person in need or pain. How would Christ pray and intercede for my family and friends?

Have you experienced Christ flowing out through you today? Why not accept the wonderful life He has planned for you and begin to live Christ? That is *living free.*

"For me, to live is Christ—His life in me; and to die is gain—[the gain of the glory of eternity]." Philippians 1:21

God is saying to me:

Thoughts I'm having today:

I've shared with the Lord:

Further thoughts and prayers:

Suffering for Jesus

Philippians 1:29

Have you ever suffered for the sake of Jesus? Did you rejoice in it or did you complain and feel sorry for yourself?

Whether you have had to go without certain foods while everyone else was eating recklessly, or were misunderstood by a friend for a particular stand or conviction, you can probably identify with suffering for a cause.

Suffering, it seems, comes in degrees. Sometimes it is so mild that we don't even recognize it as suffering. They say that an itch is a mild form of pain. Some of our suffering is like that, like a mild itch—we simply scratch it and go on. But then there are the times when, even though we handle the itches very well, the real suffering is almost too much.

For example, while at a church fellowship, the food was being served. I was carefully listening to the Lord about everything to put on my plate, and walking in wonderful obedience. A minister walked over and looked at my plate and said, "Is *that* all you are eating?" I responded with a little word of praise to the Lord for the weight loss I had experienced through obedience to Him. "Well," he said, "if that's all He lets you eat, I'm glad I didn't ask Him."

I was hurt. The degree of suffering moved beyond a mild itch to more like a mosquito bite! Long after the careless comment I still itched. Then I became angry. Where was the rejoicing I wanted from the brothers and sisters in my congregation? I allowed this comment to find a way into my spirit and for days I was angry. Wait a minute, I said. I can survive careless comments. When we obey, we will not necessarily be understood or supported by others. God's plan was not to spare me from situations like this but to prepare me to survive through them.

Another time I referred to the joy of being "thin." I weighed 145 pounds and was nearing my goal. A lady told me she was very offended that I called myself "thin." "You are *not* thin," she said. That really smarted and brought tears. But wait, she wasn't making the same comparison I was. She was comparing me to her, and compared to her I was not thin. I was comparing myself to what I had been—and I was *thin!*

I am not only granted the faith to believe in Jesus and what He is doing, but also the strength to endure and suffer if necessary. Just because an insensitive man thought that God was being cruel to me didn't make it a fact, and because a rude lady didn't think I was thin didn't make me fat. I chose to take the occasions for what they were—an attack of the enemy.

Suffering in behalf of the Lord always makes us stronger. Suffering does not make us martyrs. Martyrs are dead, and we're alive! We don't necessarily die for Jesus; He died for us. In the face of insults and stumblingblocks we live.

Step on your circumstances; throw away the trash people pitch at you, and get on with living! Suffering in the right context is like the fertilizer placed on the garden—it doesn't smell nice, but it surely produces wonderful fruit.

After all, we are *living free.*

"For you have been granted [the privilege] for Christ's sake not only to believe—adhere to, rely on and trust—in Him but also to suffer in His behalf." Philippians 1:29

God is saying to me:

Thoughts I'm having today:

I've shared with the Lord:

Further thoughts and prayers:

Knowing God

Philippians 3:10

What is your purpose for today? Not just the present age, but today, this very minute. Do you have purpose and direction? Why do you do the things you do?

It is true that many of us go through the motions of life with very little purpose to them. We sweep the floor because it is dirty. That is reason, but what is purpose? If we are not careful, we can end up with our only purpose in life being to keep floors clean. That can be a very shallow existence. We need more purpose to our lives than reasons. We can learn to live beyond the reasons for doing certain things, reaching to the real purpose for living.

Look with me at Philippians, chapter 3, verse 10: "That I may know Him and the power of His resurrection" (KJV). The verse says more than that in full context, but let's just meditate on that much today. "That I may know Him."

Do you realize that we can actually know God? We can really know Jesus. The New International Version says it like this: "Now we have moved into the area of wanting to know Jesus." How determined are we to really *know* Him?

The Amplified Version adds even more insight: My determined purpose is that I may know Him—more deeply, more intimately, and to recognize and understand Him more strongly and more clearly then ever before. That, my friend, is purpose. When we look at daily, routine things with the express purpose of allowing these activities to give us clearer understanding and knowledge of God, the mundane becomes the miraculous!

A shiny clean window can remind us of how we are to be clean and transparent before our Savior, Jesus Christ. It can remind us of 1 John, chapter 1, which tells us that by confessing our sins we can be cleansed and forgiven. A clean, orderly house can speak to us of the orderliness of God and can even reassure us that He can keep everything in order and under control just as He enables us to keep our surroundings in order.

Cleaning out the children's closets and discarding worn-out clothing can remind us that in Christ, old things are passed away, all things have become new. This reminds me that unless old things are passed away, there is not room for the new. It makes it easier for me to let old habits and attitudes go, providing space in my heart for new, fresh attitudes and habits to form.

You see? When our determined purpose is to know Jesus, more intimately, we can look at all of life as an example which confirms His work in us. Our belief in God can be strengthened by whatever we do if we seek to find Him on the everyday level of life. Life takes on purpose when the mission to know Him more today than yesterday is ever before us.

The beauty of God is that no matter how deeply you probe, how diligently you seek and search Him out, you will never exhaust the riches of His personality. Knowing God is *living free.*

"[For my determined purpose is] that I may know Him—that I may progressively become more deeply and intimately acquainted with Him, perceiving and recognizing and understanding [the wonders of His Person] more strongly and more clearly. And that I may in that same way come to know the power outflowing from His resurrection [which it exerts over believers]; and that I may so share His sufferings as to be continually transformed [in spirit into His likeness even] to His death." Philippians 3:10

God is saying to me:

Thoughts I'm having today:

I've shared with the Lord:

Further thoughts and prayers:

Measuring Up

Philippians 3:12-14

There are days when I get so wrapped up in my own short-comings—when all I seem to see in the mirror is how much I need to improve upon just to become average. I feel negative about *myself,* and because of that attitude, I find a negative attitude toward life in general creeping over me. Does this ever happen to you?

Say, for example, that one day you have a *bad* day. You are trying to watch your diet, staying within the calorie limit you feel the Lord has given you and you blow it. You go out for lunch with some friends and give in to sharing a dessert with someone. You already have eaten too much, but the idea of sharing a piece of pie doesn't sound as bad as having a *whole* piece.

When suppertime comes you think about having a salad to make up for what you ate at lunch, but then the thought invades, "What's the use of trying to rescue the day now? You've already blown it. Go ahead, eat what you want, you can try again tomorrow." That idea leads to more temptation during the evening hours.

The next day finds you standing in front of the mirror, even before breakfast, staring straight into the eyes of a "total failure." As you step on the bathroom scale the worst is confirmed. A weight gain! "Oh, well," you sigh, "I had it coming." The day begins with wrong thinking and you decide to eat donuts for breakfast instead of your responsible, balanced food plan. "I'll never make it," you moan.

There is a way out of these traps. It is the Word of God. Instead of speaking negative nuggets to yourself, making it worse, confess the truth of the situation in light of the Scriptures.

Look at Philippians, chapter 3, verses 12-14. Tell yourself the truth based on what God says about the whole situation. This is the truth; this is what I speak to myself, "Even if I have not made my goal, or am not yet what I want to be, I choose to press on to lay hold of my goals by faith because Jesus has laid hold of me and made me His own. I choose to look away from what I did yesterday and to even forgive myself, and forget those things that are in the past. I choose now to look forward to what lies ahead and what I am becoming. I choose to press on toward the goal to win the supreme and heavenly prize to which God in Christ Jesus is calling me upward."

Don't look down on yourself, look up to God. Instead of measuring yourself by your behavior and shortcomings, measure up to God's Word.

Let God speak to you about a new fresh day. You can leave yesterday in the past and not let it ruin today. How? By confessing your sins and failures to a loving Father, receiving His forgiveness, forgiving yourself, and standing on the Word of God which leads you ahead, not back.

Focusing your attention on the Word of God instead of yourself is the way to live in the spirit, *living free.*

"Not that I have now attained [this ideal] or am already made perfect, but I press on to lay hold (grasp) and make my own, that for which Christ Jesus, the Messiah, has laid hold of me and made me His own. I do not consider, brethren, that I have captured and made it my own [yet]; but one thing I do—it is my one aspiration: forgetting what lies behind and straining forward to what lies ahead, I press on toward the goal to win the [supreme and heavenly] prize to which God in Christ Jesus is calling us upward." Philippians 3:12-14

God is saying to me:

Thoughts I'm having today:

I've shared with the Lord:

Further thoughts and prayers:

God's Will

Philippians 4:4-8

Have you ever wondered if it were possible to live in the will of God every minute of the day? Have you longed to be a 100% Christian 100% of the time?

In Philippians, chapter 4, we find such clear-cut instructions that you could almost call it a "formula" for everyday life.

The beginning of the chapter is a call to unity with fellow-believers—helping one another, being of assistance wherever possible, in a true spirit of unity as in a family. Next, is the exhortation to maintain an attitude of rejoicing. Not just some of the time, but all of the time. Forsake the way of the anxious and fretful. When we remember that the Lord is near, we can be assured of His loving and sustaining hand in the middle of the most trying circumstances. Rejoicing in Him while we talk to Him about the details of our problems and being thankful that He is able and willing to do something about them is the way out of fretting and anxiety.

I received a letter from a lady in Wisconsin who reported that she had a terrific week. She had counted every calorie she had put into her mouth, and had disciplined herself to get up a little earlier every day for her morning quiet time. She had such a victorious week and then . . . she ate something she knew she shouldn't have, which made her feel guilty, which led to feeling like she had failed, and that led to eating more!

This was the day of her Overeaters Victorious meeting and she was to be responsible for sharing the lesson of the week. She felt awful! She was expected to bring encouragement to the others while she felt herself to be a failure.

Or was she?

We are the determining factor in whether or not our week is ruined by one step of disobedience. It is our interpretation of what we have done that affects the outcome.

We are admonished how to handle such situations in verse

8. "Whatever is true, whatever is noble, whatever is right, whatever is pure, whatever is lovely, whatever is admirable— if anything is excellent or praiseworthy, think about such things." Think about the positive in your life instead of the negative. You may not have *lost* any weight this week, but did you gain? You may not have uttered that kind word you could have, but did you use the cutting sarcasm that you used to? Instead of looking at how far you have to go, sometimes it is important to look at how far you have come.

Instead of allowing Satan to trick her into giving up, my friend in Wisconsin chose God's way instead, and ended the binge. Being tolerant of her mistakes in light of the progress she had made only encouraged her to bring the overeating to an end.

Take a moment to think about the true things, the noble things, the pure things, the victorious moments, the admirable qualities being developed in you. Instead of thinking about those extra pounds, remember the beauty you possess.

This is *living free.*

"Rejoice in the Lord always—delight, gladden yourselves in Him; again I say, Rejoice! [Ps. 37:4.] Let all men know and perceive and recognize your unselfishness—your considerateness, your forbearing spirit. The Lord is near—He is coming soon. Do not fret or have any anxiety about anything, but in every circumstance and in everything by prayer and petition [definite requests] with thanksgiving continue to make your wants known to God. And God's peace [be yours, that tranquil state of a soul assured of its salvation through Christ, and so fearing nothing from God and content with its earthly lot of whatever sort that is, that peace] which transcends all understanding, shall garrison and mount guard over your hearts and minds in Christ Jesus. For the rest, brethren, whatever is worthy of reverence and is honorable and seemly, whatever is just, whatever is pure, whatever is lovely and lovable, whatever is kind and winsome and gracious, if there is any

virtue and excellence, if there is anything worthy of praise, think on and weigh and take account of these things—fix your minds on them." Philippians 4:4-8

God is saying to me:

Thoughts I'm having today:

I've shared with the Lord:

Further thoughts and prayers:

Self-denial

Philippians 4:12, 13

Whenever we think of self-denial we tend to think of self-imposed punishment. As least I do. But I have had my thinking changed by reading a small article written by a medical doctor. In this article, which I read several years ago, the doctor pointed out that *to live with less to eat is really to take good care of one's body*—quite the opposite of the view typical of our culture.

When a child is sick, the typical American mother says, "Here, eat something, you'll feel better." When a teenage daughter faces an emotional crisis, whether it be a problem with a boyfriend or a final exam, mothers tend to respond with, "Here, sweetheart, eat a little something, you'll feel better."

When a family member expresses, "I'm a little tired," someone in the group counters with the suggestion: "Perhaps you need to eat a little more."

In my own situation there are always several well-meaning friends or relatives who always ask: "Are you sure you are eating enough?"

The Scripture does not tell us that the answer to life's problems are found in food. In fact, we are told more times to fast than we are to eat. In our country, going without food is a voluntary issue for the most part. We do not go without because we don't have enough. Most of us manage to fill our stomachs several times a day.

Look at Philippians, chapter 4, verses 12-13: "I have learned the secret of being content in any and every situation, whether well fed or hungry, whether living in plenty or in want."

Now here is the secret: "I can do everything through Him who gives me strength." The secret is in Jesus. Dying to the flesh and being resurrected in Him—not dwelling on our weakness, but on His strength is the answer. Not focusing on our needs but on His sufficiency. We need to stop thinking about how hungry we are, and ask instead if we are full of the

Holy Spirit. We can keep from eating too much food by feeding our spiritual being with the Word of God.

As a Christian living a life dedicated to Him, why not begin now to deny yourself some of the extravagant over-indulgences that dull your view of Him? Why not try to return to a more simple existence, rich in the presence of God? God can live through us in abundance if we let Him. He will accept the simplicity of our faith, made alive in Him, by His Word.

Try it; begin today. Move into a life where you are truly *living free.*

"I know how to be abased and live humbly in straitened circumstances, and I know also how to enjoy plenty and live in abundance. I have learned in any and all circumstances, the secret of facing every situation, whether well-fed or going hungry, having a sufficiency and to spare or going without and being in want. I have strength for all things in Christ Who empowers me—I am ready for anything and equal to anything through Him Who infuses inner strength into me, [that is, I am self-sufficient in Christ's sufficiency]." Philippians 4:12, 13

God is saying to me:

Thoughts I'm having today:

I've shared with the Lord:

Further thoughts and prayers:

Giving

Philippians 4:19

Are all your needs being met? Can you look around you and say, I have need of nothing?

In Philippians, chapter 4, Paul wrote to a New Testament congregation making them this promise: "MyGod shall supply all your needs according to His riches in glory." (KJV) This promise is for us today as well. Let's explore the promise from the context of scripture, but also from the perspective of your need. What do you need today? Paul didn't specify and categorize saying some needs will be met and others will not. He said *all* your needs.

At first glance this verse seems to be a sort of free ticket to everything, doesn't it? But wait a minute. Notice the passage beginning with verse 14: It appears that the church had sent offerings to Paul more than once. They had relieved his suffering, or as Paul puts it, affliction. How then could Paul assure them that God would supply all their needs when by his own admission here he had at times done without? It was because Paul didn't look to circumstances for the supply of his needs, but to God. His confidence was in God to supply in due time and as He willed even if it meant sometimes going without.

Paul was grateful to the people who sent him offerings for two reasons: his own relief, of course, but also, in verse 17, because of "the profit which increases to their account." Paul knew that givers become receivers—that those who send relief are also relieved. He tells them here that sowers are reapers. There is a connection between giving and blessing. By giving to Paul in the name of the Lord they were opening the channel of God's blessing upon themselves. He describes their gifts as a fragrant aroma, an acceptable sacrifice, well pleasing to God.

When we give and relieve another's suffering, we are actually being used by God, involved with the Almighty, intimately and actively included in His plans.

It is in this context that Paul states, "My God shall supply all your needs. . . ." His faith was strengthened by the fact that God had just supplied his own needs once more, giving him the practical experience to reinforce his declaration. He knew firsthand what he was talking about.

Paul knew about giving and receiving. He poured out his own life for Jesus, just as Jesus had poured out His life for him. By giving he was a sower, and when God supplied his needs through the hands of others, he not only became a reaper of souls but also had his physical needs met.

So what is your need today? You will receive in accordance with how you have given. Just reach out and meet someone else's needs, and you will see this principle working in your own life. God will supply your needs, to the full, according to His riches in glory, in harmony with the teaching of His Word. There is never a supply shortage, but there may be a giving shortage.

Robert Schuller says, "Find a need and fill it, and you will be an instant success." Why? Because it is the principle of Philippians 4. Give, and it will be given unto you—giving of ourselves, our material resources, and our time. This is the formula for *living free*.

"And my God will liberally supply (fill to the full) your every need according to His riches in glory in Christ Jesus." Philippians 4:19

God is saying to me:

Thoughts I'm having today:

I've shared with the Lord:

Further thoughts and prayers:

Hope from Hebrews

Have you ever felt as though you couldn't see the end of the tunnel? Have you felt that all the miracles happen to everyone else? Does it seem like God answers everyone else's prayers? Have you stopped praying because of these doubts? If so, this chapter is for you. You need hope—and it is promised to you. It is a gift from God; it is yours. Pick up the Bible and indulge yourself in the Word of God. Even if you don't feel hopeful now, you will. When your hope is founded in Him, based on His Word, the Father will allow you the wonderful peace that accompanies such a hope. Do not suppress it; go ahead and *dare* to hope, based on His Word.

The Word of God

Hebrews 6:12

Have you ever felt dry spiritually? In times of discouragement and satanic attack, it is so important to have the Word of God *in* us. We need it to resist the enemy during these times. Consider Hebrews, chapter 6, verse 12.

First, let me give you a little background. I had been seeking the Lord's direction in my ministry. The decisions pending would affect my personal life as well as my public life. I constantly sought God, I read His Word whenever I sat down, even if it was for a moment. When I was driving, I would either be praying or listening to the Bible on tape. I needed to have just the right direction. Every time I thought that I had a special word, I asked the Lord for a sign, for more confirmation. I was not leaving room for any errors—but neither did I leave any room for faith, or trust. I became saturated with the Word of God, but because I was listening for only one thing, one direction, one word, my prayer life became stale, and the Word of God, instead of being alive and exciting, became dead and cold. I put the Bible down, and I ceased to pray aloud.

My problem changed from a need of direction to a need of resurrection. My spirit became like a raisin—shriveled and dry. I was homesick, yet I was home. I couldn't figure it out. Then one day the realization hit—I missed God. I picked up my Bible and tried to read. How could I regain the vitality I had before? Then I recalled a verse that said in part: "so that you may not be sluggish."

Sluggish—that's what I was! I got out my Bible, paraphrased the verse into the first person and began to read it to myself. I used the Amplified Bible for reference. Over and over I said, "I am not a disinterested person or a sluggard in spiritual things, but I am a person of faith and I behave like a person of faith. I lean my entire personality on God, in Christ, in absolute trust and confidence in His power, wisdom and goodness. God promised that from my innermost being would come rivers of living water. By the practice of patient endurance I am now inheriting what God has promised me."

It didn't happen overnight. It took about three weeks, but God's Word, His wonderful Word, worked a miracle and brought me out of dryness to abundant life. Where are you today? Need a refreshing? Try Hebrews 6:12. God's Word is given to help us to *live free.*

"In order that you may not grow disinterested and become [spiritual] sluggards but imitators, behaving as do those who through faith [that is, by their leaning of the entire personality on God in Christ in absolute trust and confidence in His power, wisdom and goodness], and by practice of patient endurance and waiting are [now] inheriting the promises." Hebrews 6:12

God is saying to me:

Thoughts I'm having today:

I've shared with the Lord:

Further thoughts and prayers:

Direction and Security

Hebrews 6:17

"If what I am doing is really the will of God, why isn't everything going along without any trouble?" Did you ever think like this?

When I think about the circumstances of my life, right now, today, and I look at the outward signs, the signs that tell me to quit, I am tempted to question God's will.

If you could see the decisions that face me, the trials that await me every day, you might counsel me to simply resign and do something else—get a job in a store, work in an office, or take some classes and be trained to do something more productive.

A caring, loving, close friend said to me once, "Neva, you don't need this hassle. It's not good for you. Your health may be affected; you live under such stress. The ministry is not a good place to be. Why don't you just leave it alone and just be an ordinary person like the rest of us?"

Sometimes my own mother looks at me and says, "Daughter, you are working too hard." And my reply is simply, "Mom, could I do less?" She really knows me and has, herself, been the major influence in my life. She nods and smiles, and finally says, "I know you wouldn't do less than give it everything you have and I'm proud of you."

So what is it that keeps me going? Why do I work when others might retreat? Why do I keep going when what I really would like to do is quit? Because of a very simple verse in Hebrews: "God's plan and purpose for me is a sure and unchangeable fact." God called me into the ministry and in the ministry I will stay. God called me to do a work and I will do it. Circumstances change, situations vary, sometimes by the hour. I can't rely on what circumstances and situations tell me to do. But God's will is secure; it never changes. I will continue to do what he tells me to do. What kind of ministry am I in? I'm ministering to Him by ministering to others in His name. I don't have to have a college degree to do that . . . I just need Him.

The *way* I carry out my ministry may change; in fact, it has many times, but His plan and purpose for me stays constant. I will keep on with what He has for me to do. This is a sure and dependable way to live . . . in God's will.

How about you? In the midst of uncertain circumstances and trials of every sort, do you have something sure to hang onto? If you seek God's will for your life, by asking Him to reveal it to you, you can have the same sense of direction and security that I have. You can know the sure and unchangeable will of God.

This is the absolute way to *live free.*

"Accordingly God also, in His desire to show more convincingly and beyond doubt, to those who were to inherit the promise, the unchangeableness of His purpose and plan, intervened (mediated) with an oath." Hebrews 6:17

God is saying to me:

Thoughts I'm having today:

I've shared with the Lord:

Further thoughts and prayers:

Keeping Promises

Hebrews 6:18

Did anyone ever tell you that they would do something for you that needed to be done, and then they didn't do it? Did anyone ever promise you something and then break that promise? Were you ever lied to? Did you ever count on someone for support, and then just when you needed it you found that your friend was not in a position to give that support? Did you ever read a brochure about a vacation spot, and when you got there found that the modern cabin in the photograph was the only one at the place and it was occupied? And the only tree on the whole resort was in the view of the camera when the picture was taken? If any of these situations ring a bell with you, then you know what it is like to be disillusioned or deceived.

Deception—what a disabling, evil element. Falsehood, misrepresentation, fabrication, dishonesty, fraud—all synonymous with deception. I have used these words to illustrate what God is not. The reason it is so hard to believe God is that we are so accustomed to living with the absolute opposite of His character all around us. We tend to be skeptical because of past experiences. We want everything proven to us before we believe. Why? Because we may have believed something once too often, and been deceived one time too many. We are more acquainted with lies than truth. Did you ever hear the old saying, "Believe nothing that you hear and only half of what you see"? Things are not always what they appear to be.

God knows that we are more apt to be skeptical than believing. Yet we remain gullible and vulnerable. He knows that even with the intense conditioning most of us have had, we want to believe. We need to believe. We are immensely relieved when we find an honest friend whom we can trust. God can be to us that friend. Listen to His words to us from Hebrews, chapter 6, verse 18: "It is impossible for God to deceive me." Think about it—*impossible*. When God makes a prom-

102

ise, you can count on Him to keep it!

All things are possible with God, but deception is impossible for God. What has God promised you? Eternal life, freedom, answers to prayer, His Word, success, health, His presence, direction—the list could go on and on. Think about what God has promised you. Write them down. He cannot lie. When God makes a promise, you can place your hope in that promise. Because God cannot deceive me or ever prove to be false in His promise to me, I can flee to Him for refuge and have mighty indwelling strength and strong encouragement to grasp and hold fast the hope appointed for me and set before me.

Keep the promises of God before you. Don't let them go. Remind yourself of God's Word according to your need and then pay attention, not to the need, but to the promise. I believe from the Word of God that it is impossible for God not to fulfill His promises. When God makes a promise it is done. That's final. That's hope. That's *living free.*

"This was so that by two unchangeable things [His promise and His oath], in which it is impossible for God ever to prove false or deceive us, we who have fled [to Him] for refuge might have mighty indwelling strength and strong encouragement to grasp and hold fast the hope appointed for us and set before [us]." Hebrews 6:18

God is saying to me:

Thoughts I'm having today:

I've shared with the Lord:

Further thoughts and prayers:

Dare to Hope

Hebrews 6:19

"Can you bake this cake all by yourself?" I asked my daughter. "I think so," she answered. But she was unsure.

"Can you ride alone if I let go of the bike?" "I don't know," my son replied. He was unsure.

When I was first asked to speak to a women's group I responded with, "I'll have to get back to you about this." I was unsure. The first thing to be considered was, did I have that particular time free? Then, did I have the ability, and finally, did I have the confidence? Uncertainty. Because we are unsure of so many things in our daily lives, we may carry the uncertainty over into our relationship with God.

I asked a woman once, "Do you know Jesus?"

"Yes," she replied, "He is God's Son."

"No," I corrected, "not do you know *who* He is, but do you know *Him*?"

"Well," she hesitated, "I have read about Him, studied the Bible; I know He was a good man and lived a sinless life."

"Not enough," I said. "You know about Him, but do you know Him?"

"I'm not sure," she admitted.

"When you die, will you be going to heaven?"

"I think so," she said. "I sure hope so." But she was unsure.

Having confidence as a result of our *hope* is much more to be desired than hoping for something that we know nothing about.

Do you have the hope described in Hebrews, chapter 6, verse 19? Are you sure of your final destiny, confident of eternal life? Does your hope hold you up, or does it waver now and then? If you are constantly having to hold up and support your hope, then your hope is misplaced. Your hope should support *you*. The Bible says that hope is a sure and steadfast anchor. Move and live in hope. Fight hopelessness and despair as you would an army of ants that invade your kitchen in the summertime. Guard and hold precious your hope, protect it by reading God's Word, letting the renewing power of His Holy Spirit minister to you even in the most hopeless of times. Dare to hope; be courageous, trusting in God. Some days it will be the only thing you have. Do not let it go.

"[Now] we have this [hope] as a sure and steadfast anchor of the soul—it cannot slip and it cannot break down under whoever steps out upon it—[a hope] that reaches farther and enters into [the very certainty of the Presence] within the veil [Lev. 16:2]." Hebrews 6:19

God is saying to me:

Thoughts I'm having today:

I've shared with the Lord:

Further thoughts and prayers:

A Better Way

Hebrews 7:19-22

"I can't do it! I can't get it right! It looks awful!"

My daughter in her middle teens was in tears. "Just look at my hair. I am so ugly. My hair is so straight. I curl it and comb it, and spray it, and it still looks awful. I give up!"

The tragedies of adolescence—I understand them well. That's about where I am spiritually. I fuss and fume. I try to witness and I goof; I try to hold my temper and I have a flare-up: "If I can't do it right, I won't do it at all."

Did you ever feel like this? *Trying* to be perfect is living by the letter instead of by the spirit. I live by the rules and wonder why dryness comes into my spiritual life. Sometimes I go to church because I am expected to go to church instead of because I want to go. I greet my neighbor in a friendly way, not because I am friendly, but because I am expected to be.

When our lives take on the "have-to's and should's" instead of radiating willingness and enthusiasm we have crossed the line into legalism.

When we are defeated by our own inadequacy instead of awed by God's all-sufficiency, we are living by the rules of the flesh, not in the freedom of the spirit. In times like these we need to listen to God's Word: "The law never made anything perfect." I have to remind myself of that again and again, like when I begin to obey the diet instead of the Creator. Laws and rules dash our hope. God, the ruler, the lawgiver, gives us hope. He not only gives us hope, but guarantees it through His Son. Freedom, pardon, forgiveness are all part of His agreement. Isn't that enough to make you want to praise God without ceasing? The law never made anyone perfect; it only shows me where I am *not* like Him. But, I don't have to be perfect to come to God; I come to Him because *He* is perfect. He will take me as I am, then mold me and make me to be more and more like himself.

"Therefore He is able also to save to the uttermost—completely, perfectly, finally and for all time and eternity—those who come to God through Him, since He is always living to make petition to God and intercede with Him, and intervene for them." Hebrews 7:25

God is saying to me:

Thoughts I'm having today:

I've shared with the Lord:

Further thoughts and prayers:

Release

Hebrews 9:22

When we were children, my little brother brought home a wounded bird. We didn't know how it got hurt, but it was in obvious distress. We kept it warm in a box of leaves and straw, and fed it bugs and worms. Soon the bird became stronger. One morning, my brother went to the garage and found the little bird on the floor. It had apparently tried to fly too soon and didn't get very far. This time my brother put a cover on the box. He continued to take good care of the bird, and finally one day took it outside and released it. With very little hesitation, the bird flew away. It was free again and on its own.

As a child, I was careless and broke a glass figure belonging to my mother. Burdened with guilt for my carelessness and dreading her reaction I went to her with the pieces. She scolded me for my carelessness, gave me a little lecture, but in the end she forgave me. I was free from my burden.

I worked hard in a particular subject in high school, keeping my homework assignments current. I participated in the classroom discussions and kept my grades up. When it came time for the test at the end of the quarter, those showing high scores and class participation were exempt from having to take the test. What an unexpected release!

As an adult I was once hospitalized for 21 days. I had undergone surgery, and complications had prolonged my stay. Finally the day came when I was discharged. With my husband close at my side, I walked out of the hospital to the cool November air. It had been so warm in October when I had entered that my release had an exhilarating impact on me.

Release is a wonderful feeling: let go, freed, discharged, emancipated, delivered. I have experienced a kind of release that you cannot see, but is felt in a far deeper sense than any of the ways illustrated here. The description of it is found in Hebrews, chapter 9, verse 22. By the purifying shed blood of Jesus I am released from sin and its guilt. Remission from the punishment of sin is mine through the blood of Jesus. This is true release.

If I am in bondage to my sins because of guilt, it is of my own doing. He has done everything possible to release me from the sins and shortcomings of my past. He gave His own Son, Jesus, to take my place, to die for me, to suffer the punishment for my sins and to bridge the gap between Him and me. I must accept it and believe it.

Shamu, the whale, was captured and confined to an ocean park in California. She was very unhappy, and failed after a time to make the necessary adjustment to captivity. Finally, proving that she was dangerous to herself and to the people who came to see her, she was towed out to sea to be released. She hesitated at first, as if to relinquish her chance for freedom; but then, turning away from her captors, headed out to the open sea. Freedom was hers.

What about you? Does the example of Shamu illustrate how you have responded to spiritual release, or do you return again and again to your captor? By not accepting forgiveness and release from guilt, we stay in bondage. Some of us receive God's forgiveness, but do not forgive ourselves. We are our own captors. Jesus bought complete release for us. Without it, there is no hope of *living free*.

"[In fact], under the Law almost everything is purified by means of blood, and without the shedding of blood there is neither release from sin and its guilt nor the remission of the due and merited punishment for sins."
Hebrews 9:22

God is saying to me:

Thoughts I'm having today:

I've shared with the Lord:

Further thoughts and prayers:

Hope

Hebrews 6:10, 11; 10:11

There was a time in my life when I ministered constantly to others, all the while needing to be ministered to myself. I was a real "doer" at church, a shoulder for anyone and everyone to cry on, a teacher in the Christian education department, as well as several unofficial positions and responsibilities. But several times, faced with my own needs, I found myself alone. Where was my help? Where was the shoulder for me to cry on? Have you ever had a similar experience?

How much time have you spent preparing a lesson for your Sunday or Sabbath school class, or time listening to a neighbor, or a sister or brother in the Lord, so that you could offer support and counsel? How much time does it take for you to plan your vacation, allowing for something each one in your family wants to do? What about visiting the sick? It all takes time and attention, doesn't it?

Now, with the time you have taken ministering to others in the forefront of your thoughts, consider your own needs. What are they? Financial freedom? Victory in the area of bad habits? Time for your own Bible study or personal devotions? Perhaps you need to see God answer some prayers in a very private matter. Do you give your own needs the same quality time that you give to the needs of others? I don't mean time spent in worry and fretting, but time spent in prayer and petition before the Father presenting your own needs. We may tell a trusted friend the details of our circumstance and seek help, but do we tell God and ask for His help?

A life devoted to the needs of others is only in balance when our own needs are met so that we are prepared, and in a position to help others. We can't be an encouragement to others if we are discouraged; neither can we talk about victory if we ourselves are not victorious.

I remember sharing with a friend, who wanted to quit smoking, that Jesus could do anything, and then immediately thought, "Can He?" There I sat weighing 250 pounds! The counsel to my friend was a challenge to my own heart. But later, after losing over 100 pounds, I could say the hope I had for my friend was real and worked—because I knew it did for me.

My own hope realized gives me the credibility to counsel others. Hope is ours when we are *living free.*

> *"For God is not unrighteous to forget or overlook your labor and the love which you have shown for His name's sake in ministering to the needs of the saints— His own consecrated people—as you still do. But we do [strongly and earnestly] desire for each of you to show the same diligence and sincerity [all the way through] in realizing and enjoying the full assurance and development of [your] hope until the end. . ." Hebrews 6:10, 11*
>
> *"Furthermore, every [human] priest stands [at his altar of service] ministering daily, offering the same sacrifices over and over again, which never are able to strip (from every side of us) the sins [that envelop us], and take them away." Hebrews 10:11*

God is saying to me:

Thoughts I'm having today:

I've shared with the Lord:

Further thoughts and prayers:

Free Access

Hebrew 10:19-22

Some of the earliest memories I have include sitting on my mother's lap. I couldn't get close enough to my mother. I loved her and knew her so well, that blindfolded, I could tell my mother from all others. I never feared her, but sometimes feared her reactions, or the discipline I knew she could and would administer when necessary. I also remember coming home from my grandma's house, being carried, half-asleep, by my dad. I had absolutely no fear—he was my daddy carrying me safely to my bed. I could approach either of my parents with the smallest splinter, or the simplest problem, and know I had their undivided attention.

After being married a year or two, I could approach my husband in the same way, with the same trust and clear access. Access—what a wonderful word. Free and clear access is important in any relationship—knowing that you can approach another person who is very important to you without fear of misunderstanding, and with the assurance of their tolerance and patience.

In my own home, I have free access to every room. (I respect the privacy of my children, but I do have free access to their rooms when necessary.) I put things where I want them in cupboards and closets; I choose how the furniture should be arranged. The yard is mine to plant flowers where I want them and to tend a small garden.

My son has a cat that can jump up on his lap anytime and expect to be petted and loved. He has free access to my son, and is the most contented cat I have ever seen. He is secure and sure of himself because he is loved and he knows it.

According to Hebrews, chapter 10, verses 19 through 22, I also have free access to my heavenly Father—because of Jesus. I can run right into the holy of holies, so to speak, and not be worried that the Father is taking care of something more important than what I have to tell him. I don't have to worry that He will send me out to wait my turn. He is waiting there to meet my needs, and to take care of me whenever I need Him. It is as if God looks toward the doorway of the holy of holies waiting expectantly for me, and Jesus draws back the curtain to make the way open for me to come in.

It is important that I have free access to my Father. It is in His presence that I find freedom from guilt and cleansing for my soul. When I come by faith with my heart toward God, I have free access. Not because of what I have done, but because of what Jesus has done for me. I didn't buy or earn this free access. He gave it to me. There is such freedom in living with instant and free access to the Father.

"Therefore, brethren, since we have full freedom and confidence to enter into the [Holy of] Holies by the power and virtue in the blood of Jesus, by this fresh (new) and living way which He initiated and dedicated and opened for us through the separating curtain [veil of the Holy of Holies], that is, through His flesh; and since we have such a great and wonderful and noble Priest [Who rules] over the house of God, let us all come forward and draw near with true (honest and sincere) hearts in unqualified assurance and absolute conviction engendered by faith, [that is, by that leaning of the entire personality on God in absolute trust and confidence in His power, wisdom and goodness,] having our hearts sprinkled and purified from a guilty (evil) conscience and with our bodies cleansed with pure water." Hebrews 10:19-22

God is saying to me:

Thoughts I'm having today:

I've shared with the Lord:

Further thoughts and prayers:

Assurance

Hebrews 11:1

Faith is the assurance of things hoped for, and hope means confidence, expectation, trust, belief, desire, anticipation, optimism, and reliance. There is no passivity in hope. It is active belief in a positive reality.

I have known people who hope and hope and hope and yet nothing happens. Others I know, hope, and everything they hope for happens. What makes the difference? The basis for their hope. Godly, scripturally based hope is not presumption. Listen to these comments from my mail: "Four years ago I lost 47 pounds through memorizing scriptures that deal with temptation, the flesh, etc. I have now gained back 30 pounds and am constantly trying to start over, lose again, and conquer the flesh! I am a pastor's wife, and have so many extra dinners, luncheons, and coffees that I must attend. I am discouraged, desperate, and at times without hope at all that I can ever overcome and be thin again!"

An expression of hope? Not quite! But listen to this one: "I have been thanking God every day since He led me to read your book *Free To Be Thin*. I wanted to let you know that this book has given me hope for the first time in several years. I had been a slave to my appetite until God answered my prayers through your book. Thank you for sharing. I know God will continue to support and encourage me in my new eating habits. All the glory goes to God, as I report a weight loss of 13 pounds already. What a victory! I had given up all hope of ever attaining my goal, but now I am confident that I can lose another 87 pounds!"

What is the difference between these letters? Hebrews, chapter 11, verse 1. Faith is the *assurance* of the things hoped for.

Both of these ladies have hope; they are both born-again Christians, but one of them has claimed and received assurance! Assurance makes the difference. Receiving assurance of what we hope for takes time and prayer. It means staying in harmony with the Word of God, looking away from what we have done or been, to what God has done and is doing right now and will continue to do for us in the future.

Hoping without assurance from God, found in His Word, is like living a fantasy. Hoping without a real foundation for our hope is not reality. But faith is the assurance, the substance, the ingredients of what we hope for.

"My faith is the assurance of the things I hope for. . . ." Take a pound of hamburger, an egg, spices, a little oatmeal and an onion. Place it on the counter, and ask my husband what it is. . . . He'll just shrug unless he knows that I am making a meatloaf. You and I know what is already in our minds and plans—a meatloaf, or whatever. "It is the proof of things I do not see and convicts me of their reality. . . ." Even before we put the meatloaf into the oven we are planning the vegetable and other dishes to complement the meatloaf. ". . . My faith perceives as real fact what is not yet revealed to my senses. . . ." Even before I smell the meatloaf baking, I know that it is meatloaf, because I had the right ingredients and I put them together.

What are your ingredients for hope today? Do you have faith in a Father who is ready and willing to help you? He wants you to be *living free* more than you do.

"Now faith is the assurance (the confirmation, the title-deed) of the things [we] hope for, being the proof of things [we] do not see and the conviction of their reality—faith perceiving as real fact what is not revealed to the senses." Hebrews 11:1

God is saying to me:

Thoughts I'm having today:

I've shared with the Lord:

Further thoughts and prayers:

Gems from James

James is a book full of rich spiritual truth and treasure. The verses speak of principles, and the work of God in the hearts and lives of His people. James is a book that reveals the secrets of successful Christian living by giving us some formulas. For instance, the formula for acquiring wisdom is found here, and the way to resist the devil. The "Hows" and "Whys" of trials and testings are given. The importance of our works, the law of liberty and patience are all addressed in James. James is a very enlightening part of the Bible, giving us the *practicals* of the victorious life. It is really all about living free! I suggest you take these verses and apply them to your everyday life.

Steadfastness

James 1:2-4

Two things I have found I need in order to be an overcomer are steadfastness and endurance. Think about it. Picture two men in separate circumstances. One is walking down a smooth path without stones or obstacles. There is a fine, gray, misty fog that parts right before him as he walks. It is early morning, the air is cool, but not chilly; the trees are barely rustling overhead in the ever-so-light breeze. You can hear the birds chirping and smell the roses along the side of the path. What a wonderful setting in which to pray, and wonder at the goodness and mercy of the Lord.

The other man has been walking along quite another path. It ascends almost straight up at times. It is narrow, and often strewn with rocks and broken branches. It leads to the top of a mountain, which cannot be seen. It winds and twists, sometimes barely a few inches wide, slippery in spots, and dropping straight off to a raging sea below. It is raining, and dense fog keeps visibility at zero. The man along this path has slipped and fallen on a rock, and is hanging onto the side of the cliff. He is shouting for help, but no one hears him. He knows that if he can just hang on, the storm will soon subside, the rocks will dry, he will be able to see better, and the chances of his survival will improve. *If* he just hangs on.

Now which of these two men needs endurance? Which of the two needs to encourage himself with positivie words about his ability to endure? Which of the men will come out of his respective circumstance with more confidence? Which will be the stronger, richer, and wiser?

James, chapter 1, verses 2 through 4, tells us to count or consider it joy when we fall into the various trials and temptations that come our way in this life. When we have a choice of paths, we all tend toward the smooth, easy way. We want to start on the journey of experience, reassured that God has removed the obstacles. We need to be convinced of the safety of the plotted course. And yet, the Bible tells us that difficult times are essential for growth and maturity. We say we have faith, yet shrink from any experience that might test and prove that faith.

God's Word encourages us to be daring. Go ahead and do that thing which seems impossible, that God has been asking you to do. It will actually prove that you are what you say you are. Let endurance and steadfastness be built into you. Let your backbone be strengthened, and your inner-self be reinforced. Why? Verse 4: "So that you may be people perfectly and fully developed with no defect, lacking in nothing." We are here to get a job done. We need to be fully equipped to do that job. We are called the army of the Lord. Let us leave training maneuvers and exercises, and get into the real battle! This is not a game but a war . . . we are the soldiers; the almighty God is our Captain.

We don't need to have all the paths made smooth and flat. If we are spiritually prepared we can tackle every situation as though the path *were* smooth and flat. We don't need to have every problem solved ahead of time; with the mind and ability of God flowing through us, we are able to face and solve problems as they come. We are ready if we have learned through our experience to trust and hang onto God's Word. We can have joy in the face of the most severe testing, in the time of temptation and trial. Our joy is not dependent on circumstances—we are *living free*.

"Consider it wholly joyful, my brethren, whenever you are enveloped in or encounter trials of any sort, or fall into various temptations. Be assured and understand that the trial and proving of your faith bring out endurance and steadfastness and patience. But let endurance and steadfastness and patience have full play and do a thorough work, so that you may be [people] perfectly and fully developed (with no defects), lacking in nothing." James 1:2-4

126

God is saying to me:

Thoughts I'm having today:

I've shared with the Lord:

Further thoughts and prayers:

Wisdom

James 1:5-8

"What shall I do?" "How should I respond?" "Which way should I go?" These are everyday questions asked verbally or in the mind by everyone at one time or another. Making decisions is an integral part of all of our lives.

Frequently we are called upon to decide between two or more "right" things to do. If all of our decisions were based on a choice between right and wrong, the issue would be simple. Let me illustrate. We are daily faced with simple choices: "Should I wear the yellow dress or the blue one? Either would be appropriate, both suit the season and the weather, but which shall I wear?"

Maybe you don't find this level of decision-making very difficult, but many do. Some can cope with the major decisions of life, but find simple choices impossible to make. There are those who spend so much time struggling over simple choices that they have expended all their energy and can't face the major decisions of life. Fussing with trivia exaggerates its importance.

I have found the same to be true in choices of food. "Should I eat an egg or another source of protein for breakfast?" At times it becomes such an issue that I have grown weary (and hungry) in the process, and finally eaten a sweet roll simply because I could not decide between two "rights."

"Should I eat meat, or just vegetables?" "Should I use diet products, or not?" "Should I serve chicken or beef to my guests?" Many decisions, which in the long run will make little difference, weigh heavily upon me. How can we learn to make the simple decisions of life? Let's look at James 1:5-8.

God's wisdom is not necessarily reserved for the weighty, critical issues of life, but is given liberally to all who ask in faith to be applied in the matters that face us every day. If something is particularly hard for you to decide about, you need to realize that God's wisdom is available to you for just that matter—not because the issue is necessarily important to God, but because *you* are. You can apply His wisdom to the most simple of all life's situations. There is no end to God's wisdom just as there is no end to His forgiveness. But we do need to ask, in faith, for wisdom from above.

Let the Word of God from this passage in James make its way into your spirit. Change your way of thinking; God's wisdom is made available to you—it's yours. God won't make the decisions for you, but He does give you the wisdom and ability to make them yourself. Either way, the glory is still His. Those walking in the wisdom of God are *living free.*

> *"If any of you is deficient in wisdom, let him ask of the giving God [Who gives] to every one liberally and ungrudgingly, without reproaching or faultfinding, and it will be given him. Only it must be in faith that he asks, with no wavering—no hesitating, no doubting. For the one who wavers (hesitates, doubts) is like the billowing surge out at sea, that is blown hither and thither and tossed by the wind. For truly, let not such a person imagine that he will receive anything [he asks for] from the Lord, [for being as he is] a man of two minds— hesitating, dubious, irresolute—he is unstable and unreliable and uncertain about everything (he thinks, feel, decides)." James 1:5-8*

God is saying to me:

Thoughts I'm having today:

I've shared with the Lord:

Further thoughts and prayers:

Endurance

James 1:12

In the State of California there is a proficiency test that all students must pass before they can graduate from high school. The first time the test is given officially is in the ninth grade. If the student passes the test, he doesn't have to take it again, but can proceed with his elected course of direction and the educational studies geared to his career goals.

Some students start practicing by actually taking the test as early as the seventh grade. At this early date, these students are not expected to pass the test, but use it to show themselves in what areas they are weak. Their educational goals are set accordingly, as they prepare to take the test again the following spring. It is not a test that can be studied for, because it only determines how much the student has learned in each subject up to that point. The test can be given up to five years early of the actual time it should be passed. This gives the student time to learn, to correct, strengthen, and fill in any gaps in his progress in time to graduate on schedule.

Two of my children have taken this test—one as a ninth-grader, and the other a seventh-grader. The ninth-grade student was nervous and anxious at the time of the test. For days she wondered and worried, even after I had explained the function of the test, as I have here. Ordinarily she is not upset by exams and tests; she simply studies and does her best. But in this case she was bothered because there was nothing to study, no way to prepare for it. Her educational development was about to be tested, and she felt helpless and not in control of the situation.

My other child's attitude was quite the reverse. She is the one who is usually very anxious and apprehensive at exam time. But for this test she simply relaxed and did what she could. The difference? She knew that seventh-graders are not expected to pass the test. She knew that she had two more years before she would actually be expected to have a high score.

Think about my homely example, as you think about James, chapter 1, verse 12. The tests we have in this life have eternal value. Our attitude toward the tests we go through determines how we will react to more testing in the future. Tests of our faith, commitment, determination, and character show our spiritual development, our proficiency in spiritual matters. These tests prepare us for days ahead.

Can God trust wealth to one who has not learned the difference between the basics and the extras? Could God trust you with a thin body without the tendency to gain again, or would you then become independent and forget your commitment to Him? Could God really bring you into full health if He knew that walking in it would rob you of your sensitivity toward those who do not have it? Tests directly related to the promise God has given you does not keep you from receiving the promise, but will determine whether or not you are ready for it.

We may approach these tests much the same as my anxious ninth-grader, not sure that we have the wherewithal to meet such a test. But how will you know if you shun the test? If you fail, you will be given time for correction and strength, and then the test will be given again. Remember, this is not a pass/fail situation, but a measure of development and growth. We will never experience total defeat if we keep our attitudes right. We are intact; we are not falling apart, but the stuff with which we are held together is being tested. Let the test have its full work, let it reveal areas of need and weakness. We are being prepared for greater, more glorious things ahead.

"Blessed, happy, to be envied is the man who is patient under trial and stands up under temptation, for when he has stood the test and been approved he will receive [the victor's] crown of life which God has promised to those who love Him." James 1:12

God is saying to me:

Thoughts I'm having today:

I've shared with the Lord:

Further thoughts and prayers:

Obligations

James 1:22-25; 2:12

There are so many obligations in life, and many are self-imposed. We ought to go to church everytime the doors are open. We ought to take food to the family grieving the loss of a loved one. We ought to be home when our children arrive from school. We ought to drive a neighbor to the store. We ought to call Aunt Martha at least once a month. We ought to have a daily quiet time. The list could go on and on, and your list of "oughts" may vary from mine, but probably not too much. "Oughts," "have-tos," "shoulds"—all negative forces, and stiflers of creativity.

Should we throw out these governors completely? Can a person really live without them? To be completely free from the "shoulds"—that would be to live only by our "want-tos." We would go to church only when we "wanted to," call Aunt Martha when we "wanted to," be home for our children when we "wanted to," have a daily quiet time when we "wanted to." "Want-tos" are closely related to "feel-like-its." The trouble with living according to "feel-like-its" is that we would be living only according to the flesh. Calling Aunt Martha only when we feel like it doesn't take into consideration her feelings or needs at all, only ours.

This motivation does not solve any problems. Think about it. It is a very rare day that an overeater wants to keep an account of the calories consumed. The overspender only wants to keep balanced books on occasion—such as when she is overdrawn at the bank.

The answer to living a productive and effective life is not found in either extreme, because the one is motivated by what we feel others want us to do, and the other by what our flesh wants us to do. The Scriptures plainly show us a better way. It is the law of liberty found in James, chapters one and two. The law of liberty makes an impressive difference. Think about your "Aunt Martha" again. Instead of calling her only when you feel like it, or on a regular schedule because you *should*, remember her in your prayers and listen to the Holy Spirit. He will prompt you to call her at the opportune time, when you can best minister to her the love of the Father. The law of liberty frees us to cooperate with the Holy Spirit. We can be accountable in this same spirit in our food intake, our time management, our spending habits and other areas of stewardship. We don't have to "be good" to prove ourselves worthy of God. It is because we are not worthy that He came to us. We no longer are "do-gooders" driven by guilt, but "good-doers" motivated by mercy.

We don't work to be acceptable to God; Jesus came and presented himself to God in our behalf because He knew we would never be acceptable. Then Jesus presented us to God, washed in His blood and cleansed, purified and made perfect in Him.

When we understand the law of liberty, we will be able to understand why instead of being driven to change the whole world, we are drawn to minister to individuals. I do not feel as driven to speak to large groups of people as much as I am drawn to love my next-door neighbor. Take the mirror of God's Word and look at it frequently throughout the day. Make sure your spirit reflects the law of liberty. Psalm 119 says: "How can a young man keep his way pure? By keeping it according to God's word." A list of rules and regulations? Commandments and conditions? Yes, if you are living by "shoulds" or "want-tos," but if you are really *living free,* you will find the law of liberty instead, which presents opportunities, not ultimatums.

"But—obey the message; be doers of the Word, and not merely listeners to it, betraying yourselves [into deception by reasoning contrary to the Truth]. For if any one only listens to the Word without obeying it and being a doer of it, he is like a man who looks carefully at his [own] natural face in a mirror; for he thoughtfully observes himself, then goes off and promptly forgets what he was like. But he who looks carefully into the fault-

less law, the [law] of liberty, and is faithful to it and perseveres in looking into it, being not a heedless listener who forgets, but an active doer [who obeys], he shall be blessed in his doing—in his life of obedience."
James 1:22-25
"So speak and so act as [people should] who are to be judged under the law of liberty [the moral instruction given by Christ, especially about love]." James 2:12

God is saying to me:

Thoughts I'm having today:

I've shared with the Lord:

Further thoughts and prayers:

Faith at Work

James 2:20-22

"Food is not my problem," a woman shared with me. "Only God knows why I am fat." "I really don't overeat," said another, who weighed in at 275 pounds. "I can't see that going on a diet will help me at all."

Some of us will read the above statements and be tempted to laugh. But some people really believe them. And there are more: "I have turned this problem of overeating over to God, and if I were to go on a diet it would be like taking the problem back into my own hands."

"My problem is not that I spend too much, but that I have too little."

"God loves me whether my house is a mess or not. So I figure, why knock myself out?"

"Witnessing? Sure, if God sees fit to bring the person across my path—if they ask me I'll tell them, but I am not the type to push Jesus down everyone's throat."

Let's look at James, chapter 2, verses 20-22: "Do you want to be shown, you shallow man, that faith apart from works is barren?" (NAS) "Are you willing to be shown proof, you foolish, unproductive, spiritually deficient fellow, that faith apart from good works is inactive and ineffective and worthless?" (AMP) "When will you ever learn that 'believing' is useless without doing what God wants you to?" (TLB)

Believing is not a passive state of thinking, or giving mental assent. Believing is actively setting our goals, our plans, and our actions according to God's Word. If you believe the Great Commission, you don't wait for opportunities to share Jesus; you make opportunities.

If you believe that Jesus has set you free according to John, chapter 8, verses 31-36, then you begin to act in that freedom as you make conscious effort to change habits and attitudes.

"Waiting for God to do it" is ridiculous; He has already done it. So stop waiting and put into personal, practical practice what He has done. He has given you freedom; now walk in that freedom. He gave you the Word to witness to others; now speak up. Go out and find a person who will listen; don't wait for them to find you.

Many people wait for God to perform a miracle for them by giving them a thin body. But remember, the thin body was what most of us started out with. It has already been done at Calvary. Did you know that? Do you live as if you knew it?

God doesn't make people fat, He sets people free. James 2:22 in the Amplified Version states: "His faith was completed and reached its supreme expression when He implemented it by good works." Dieting is not a substitute for faith—it is an expression of it.

Your problem area may not be overeating or being overweight, but whatever it is, the same principles of faith apply. In the area of spending, we don't express our faith in "God shall supply all our needs" by overspending, but by cutting down, trusting God for the money ahead of the purchase. You may not get everything you want, but you'll get all you need.

Put your faith to work today; that's the only way it will really live. Faith at work is the lifestyle of those who are *living free.*

"Are you willing to be shown [proof], you foolish, unproductive, spiritually-deficient fellow, that faith apart from [good] works is inactive and ineffective and worthless? Was not our forefather Abraham [shown to be justified—made acceptable to God—by [his] works when he brought to the altar as an offering his [own] son Isaac? [Gen. 22:1-14.] You see that his faith was co-operating with his works, and [his] faith was completed and reached its supreme expression [when he implemented it] by [good] works." James 2:20-22

God is saying to me:

Thoughts I'm having today:

I've shared with the Lord:

Further thoughts and prayers:

To Rhonda

James 3:17, 18

This is your first year of high school, and as I watch you enter this wonderful (awful) phase of your adolescence, I want you to know this from God's Word. You will need all the wisdom you can possibly gather in these next few years. There will be situations that confront you that you have not had to face before. You will not be able to draw upon experience to make your decisions, nor will you be able to simply turn and ask me what to do, for most likely, I will not always be there. What you will need is wisdom. That's a lot to ask of a sixteen-year-old, isn't it? It isn't your own wisdom you will need, however, but the wisdom referred to in James, chapter three.

The Bible tells us here that there are two kinds of wisdom. The world's wisdom and the wisdom that comes from God. Simply using common sense is not always the answer; it has to be God's wisdom. The world's wisdom will sometimes look so right, so proper and correct, but if used will only prove to be the counterfeit it is. Let me explain.

In the early days of California, there was such a gold-fever that grown men left ordinary, responsible lives, homes and families to try to get their "share" of this precious metal. Some of them were sadly disappointed when what they had really found, fought for, and hoarded was fool's gold. It looked just like gold, but it wouldn't stand the assayer's test. As much as it glittered and beckoned, it wasn't the real thing.

Actually, those men should have known there was something wrong—real gold is found in rocks, sometimes uncovered by streams of water, washing and wearing for centuries over them, but more often real gold strikes were found deep in the hills. The mines were often risky places to work, but the anticipation of wealth kept many motivated enough to endure the hardships and risk the dangers.

Fool's gold, on the other hand, was often found on the surface, just lying there glistening in the hot desert sun. Why go to all the trouble to dig and explore and work hard when any "fool" could see that the glittering rock was lying all around, just for the taking?

It's much the same with wisdom. Fool's wisdom is so easy to come by. It is all around us for the taking, and most people live by it. Why work hard and study when any "fool" can see that for a few dollars you can buy anything from answers to tests, and book reports, to pills that make you "feel better." This is "fool's gold," Rhonda. Don't settle for it, when the real thing is there if you will only establish your claim and then dig for it.

An assayer tested the metals in the old mining days. He would examine and test the miners' samples and tell them if the metal was the real thing and how pure it was. The Bible is our assayer. It will tell you how real your wisdom is if you bring your problems, questions, and decisions to the Word and measure them against it.

You will know that your decisions are "foolish" if they are made as a result of jealousy or selfish ambitions. But the wisdom from God, the "real thing," the "22-carat" wisdom is first pure . . . (unmixed, unadulterated, spotless, stainless, undefiled, innocent, immaculate, clean) then peaceable . . . (bringing calmness, quietness, serenity. It leaves you unruffled, tranquil, and composed).

God's wisdom will be gentle as opposed to forceful and urgent. It will help you stay open to reason instead of driving you to be close-minded and obstinate.

God's wisdom is so much more to be desired than the world's wisdom. It is the real thing. There are thirty-five synonyms listed for wisdom, but, my lovely daughter, there is no substitute for it. Avail yourself of the wisdom from above. Stay in God's Word and you will find that these high school days can be tremendous days of opportunity for *living free.*

Love,
Mom

"But the wisdom from above is first of all pure (undefiled); then it is peace-loving, courteous (considerate,

gentle). [It is willing to] yield to reason, full of compassion and good fruits; it is wholehearted and straightforward, impartial and unfeigned—free from doubts, wavering and insincerity. And the harvest of righteousness (of conformity to God's will in thought and deed) is [the fruit of the seed] sown in peace by those who work for and make peace—in themselves and in others, that is, that peace which means concord (agreement, harmony) between individuals, with undisturbedness, in a peaceful mind free from fears and agitating passions and moral conflicts." James 3:17, 18

God is saying to me:

Thoughts I'm having today:

I've shared with the Lord:

Further thoughts and prayers:

New Opportunities

James 4:6-10

I woke up one morning, not very enthused about the day. The day before I had nibbled my way from morning till night and I felt the physical consequences of my actions; but more important than that, I felt the heaviness of knowing that I had acted independently of the Lord. How did I deal with the guilt? I knew that I should read the Bible, and yet my enthusiasm was at an all-time low. I could have prayed, but I didn't *want* to!

Have you ever felt like this? How do we deal with today in the light of yesterday? How do we escape the heavy feeling?

Let's look into the Word of God to see what it has to say to us. In James, we are encouraged in the fourth chapter, starting with verse six: "He gives more grace. Wherefore He says, God resists the proud, but gives grace unto the humble. Submit yourselves therefore to God. Resist the devil, and he will flee from you. Draw nigh to God, and He will draw nigh to you. Cleanse your hands, you sinners: and purify your hearts, you double-minded. Be afflicted and mourn, and weep: Let your laughter be turned to mourning, and your joy to heaviness. Humble yourselves in the sight of the Lord, and He shall lift you up."

Isn't that what you need? I do. A lift. A real pick-me-up. The temptation is to say to ourselves, "I will do better today, but I will not forget what I did yesterday, because I need it as a reminder to do better today. If I carry these heavy feelings I will not soon forget. This will serve as a deterrent to bad behavior as well as a just punishment. Certainly, if I were to forget what I did yesterday, I would be forgiving myself, and I don't deserve forgiveness."

First of all, to carry the trash of yesterday into today will not help us to do better, but worse. Condemnation is not a deterrent but a guarantee that we will do as bad, or even worse. Secondly, forgiveness in never *deserved*. It is unmerited, but follows wrongdoing. Without sin, there would be no forgiveness.

First John, chapter 1, verse 9, says this: "If we confess our sins, he is faithful and just to forgive us our sins and to cleanse us from all unrighteousness" (KJV). To ask forgiveness for yesterday's shortcomings, overindulgences, or careless words, is how we humble ourselves. By reading the Bible and doing what it says, we are submitting to God. That is the first step toward a better day. By refusing condemnation, and receiving forgiveness we are actually resisting the devil. Another way to resist him is to address him directly: "I resist you, Satan, and according to God's Word you have to flee from me."

Draw nigh to God now, in quietness and the freedom of forgiveness. You are clean before the Lord. Do you sense His nearness? This very moment God is remaining true to His Word and is drawing nigh to you. Set your mind on Him and what He is doing in your heart and life. Look at the freedom He desires for you and not at the disappointing yesterdays you have had. Look toward the positive possibilities for today and tomorrow. Through confessing our sins to our gracious and loving Father, we have cleansed our hands and purified our hearts. We have humbled ourselves in the sight of God.

What is the promise then remaining for us? He shall lift you up. Will you let Him? Will you receive the freshness of new opportunities to serve God today with a clean heart? Will you walk today in the freedom of being a doer of God's Word?

This is how to recapture lost territory and once again be *living free.*

"But He gives us more and more grace [power of the Holy Spirit, to meet this evil tendency and all others fully]. That is why He says, God sets Himself against the proud and haughty, but gives grace [continually] to the lowly—those who are humble-minded [enough to receive it]. [Prov. 3:34.] So be subject to God.—Stand firm against the devil; resist him and he will flee from you. Come close to God and He will come close to you. [Recognize that you are] sinners, get your soiled hands

clean; [realize that you have been disloyal] wavering individuals with divided interests, and purify your hearts [of your spiritual adultery]. [As you draw near to God] be deeply penitent and grieve, even weep [over your disloyalty]. Let your laughter be turned to grief and your mirth to dejection and heartfelt shame [for your sins]. Humble yourselves—feeling very insignificant—in the presence of the Lord, and He will exalt you.—He will lift you up and make your lives significant." James 4:6-10

God is saying to me:

Thoughts I'm having today:

I've shared with the Lord:

Further thoughts and prayers:

Waiting Patiently

James 5:7, 8

It is discouraging to spend time, effort, and tears helping someone in difficulty and then to see them slip back and fall. If they reach out again to you for help you are hopeful, but when they go to a different source that you know is not the answer, it is even more painful.

I know how that feels; I have experienced it myself. I also know that I have been the one in need many times. I have cried out to God, and then when I felt His help slow in coming, I have turned to another source for help, only to be disappointed, and in the end having to return again to my heavenly Father.

When this happens, we have forgotten about James, chapter 5, verses 7 and 8. We are told here to wait patiently for the situation or circumstance to be turned around by the hand of God. We are told to use this time of waiting to establish our hearts. We learn that instead of giving in to all the negative signs and indicators, we can use them to reinforce our determination to follow God, His ways, and His Word. I came to this decision very recently. I told a friend, "I will take God and His Word as my help. It is God's Word or nothing."

Then when all indications pointed to giving up, when people I had counted on had disappointed me, and not measured up to what I had expected, I chose to be determined and trust God. It was not the easiest thing to do, but it was the right thing to do.

What does it mean to be patient? Patience is self-control, restraint, a strength that enables one to endure waiting, or suffering, or any unpleasant, painful period of time. It indicates a willingness to wait without becoming disgruntled or anxious.

A few weeks ago, I was sitting in the lobby of our local hospital with my mother, while my father had surgery. While waiting, we read books without really comprehending the words. We looked at magazines without seeing the pictures. Our thoughts were with Dad, but we had no choice but to wait. We went to the cafeteria and had lunch. Life went on, even though we were anxious about just one thing. Patience meant waiting, trusting that the surgeon was in control, capable and skilled.

When we can't do anything ourselves about a situation, we tend to be impatient. Patience requires trust in someone else who is better skilled than we are.

My children are assigned household chores. In this case, it takes patience on my part to allow them to do these routine duties when I could do it myself in less time and maybe more to my liking.

My daughter had braces put on her teeth. At the time, we were told they could be taken off in two years. What an eternity that seemed to her at the time. Little did she know that at the end of the two years the orthodontist would see the need to leave them on a little longer. The two years stretched into four and that took patience. Month after month she had to go in for the painful adjustment. But when her braces came off, she looked at her wonderful smile in the mirror and said, "It was worth it; it doesn't seem so long now." Quickly she forgot the tears and the pain. And more than her teeth were straightened! Her jaw line completely changed. Instead of a little pointed chin, she now has an adorable, petite round one. Now, instead of taking her teeth for granted, she has a great respect and sense of responsibility toward them. She also developed a wonderful sense of patience. As the bands of stainless steel and wires worked to correct the line of her teeth, her character was straightened and strengthened too.

We need to have a healthy outlook when some things in our life seem to take forever to work out. We need to be patient, knowing God uses the time we are waiting for His promises to be fulfilled, to make us ready for the answer. God not only grants our needs and requests, but equips us to handle that which He gives us. Patience is a characteristic to develop. What has God promised you? Wait patiently for it, and when you receive it, you will understand that the waiting was also part of the learning and the growing.

> *"So be patient, brethren, [as you wait] till the coming of the Lord. See how the farmer waits expectantly for the precious harvest from the land. [See how] he keeps up his patient [vigil] over it until it receives the early and late rains. So you also must be patient. Establish your hearts—strengthen and confirm them in the final certainty—for the coming of the Lord is very near."*
> *James 5:7, 8*

God is saying to me:

Thoughts I'm having today:

I've shared with the Lord:

Further thoughts and prayers:

Songs from Psalms

When life's trials bring depression, you can find relief in the Psalms. When life's blessings call for rejoicing, you can find personal expression in the Psalms. For every degree of human emotion from agony to ecstacy there is a Psalm.

During my quiet time, the Psalms have encouraged me, healed me, given me words with which to praise God, taught me deep truths about God's wonderful character, and revealed Jesus to me in a way unique to the Psalmist.

I hope that this series of quiet times proves to be as rich to you as the writing of it has been to me. I am more aware today of the wonder of God's love toward those who will trust Him than I have ever been before. Reach out to God through the Psalms; His promise is that He will be found.

God Is with Me

Psalm 1

My delight and desire . . .
My source of pleasure and fulfillment as well as my enjoyment of life. My hunger, my wishes, my appetites, my longings and wants . . .
Are in the Lord.
In His law, His instructions and teachings.
I love to listen to Him, sing to Him, worship Him. I allow His law of liberty to be written on my heart and be worked out in my life, in my behavior and in my habits.
I love to meditate on Him day and night.
There is nothing worth thinking about that takes my focus off Him. I choose to discipline myself to remember Him at all times, in all situations and while facing every temptation and decision. When tempted to care (be anxious) I choose instead to think about Him and His caring for me. When faced with decisions I choose to ask Him what to do. I take His Word with me and internalize it, externalize it, and digest it so that it affects every part of my life.
Everything I do shall prosper and come to maturity . . .
I do not have to fear failure, because even in times of failure or defeat I have the opportunity to learn again of God's faithfulness. Everything I do will have a measure of success as I live in responsive obedience to God in everything I do. I have the ability to see things through to a finish, fulfillment, completion. I do God's will and nothing will stop me.
For the Lord knows . . .
I do not escape His attention. He is ever watching over me as well as watching out for me. He knows what I faced yesterday, as well as what I face today and also what I will face tomorrow. He knows. Nothing that I tell Him will come as a surprise. He will not be taken unawares or unprepared to help me. He knows.

. . . and is fully acquainted . . .

He himself was tempted in every respect like I am tempted, and yet He was without sin. I do not have as my High Priest one who cannot identify with me, for He became like me, a human being, in order to help me in just such times as these. He knows from the inside out what things threaten to turn me inside out.

. . . with everything I do.

There is nothing that I do that God does not know already. I have assurance that I am not alone. I do not face trouble or trials alone. I do not count my calories alone; I do not balance my budget alone. I do not make my plans and dream my dreams alone. Everything I do is important to Him, because *I* am important to Him.

He is present,

Emmanuel, God is with me, present, beside, right here.

He is here.

In Him I live free.

Read Psalm 1

God is saying to me:

Thoughts I'm having today:

I've shared with the Lord:

Further thoughts and prayers:

Blessed

Psalm 3

Look, O Lord, what you are for me!
A shield and my glory . . .
When I am assailed by the darts and arrows of the enemy, you protect me. You give me wonderful zest for living and an inner spark. You put a spring in my step and a twinkle in my eye. In spite of the attacks of Satan, I walk unhindered and unafraid.

You lift my head . . .
In times of depression you give me hope and purpose. When tired, you refresh me. In time of faithlessness, you restore me by your faithfulness. When all others misunderstand me, you understand. When I am hated, you love me. When I sin, you forgive me. You have countless ways to lift my head, appropriate to the cause for my being downcast.

You hear and answer me when I cry to you . . .
Even when I cry in self-pity, you still comfort me. When I cry in pain, you heal me. When I cry in trouble, you rescue; when I cry for knowledge, you teach. When I cry for wisdom, you give it to me liberally. When I cry because I am lost, you give direction. You always hear my cry when I am tempted and you give me victory.

You sustain me . . .
In you I have my being. In you I have my reason for living. In you I have courage; in you I persevere and endure. With joy I make it through the day.

. . . when threatened. . . .
Either in reality or when imagined, you, O Lord, will arise and save me!

Salvation belongs to you, Lord. . . .
And because of Jesus' death upon the cross you freely give it now to me. I don't understand it, but I gratefully accept it.

Your blessing is upon me . . .
My days are blessed, my obedience is blessed, my family is

blessed, my hands are blessed, my marriage is blessed, my ministry is blessed . . .

Because I am one of your people!
Because of that, I am living free.

Read Psalm 3

God is saying to me:

Thoughts I'm having today:

I've shared with the Lord:

Further thoughts and prayers:

Praise

Psalm 9:1, 2, 11, 12

I praise you, O Lord, with my whole heart.
I watch over my heart with all diligence. I do not let anything enter my heart which discourages my praise to you. I choose the life of praise. My whole heart sings praises to you. I do not allow half-hearted praise to be my style. My attitudes are sanctified and made holy before you. I choose to have a heart perfect before you. My attitude will submit to my praises of you.

I will be a demonstration in my life of how marvelous are the workings of God in the lives of His people.
I will eat in obedience to you. I will allow myself enough rest and relaxation to be at my best for you. I will choose a balanced way of living as you show me how. I will give you glory and praise in the presence of others, and testify to the answers to prayer in my own life. I will not be in bondage to anything since you have given me freedom. I choose to walk in orderliness, forgiveness, freedom, free from care, anxiety and anger. I choose to be an example of what you can do in a life totally yielded to you. I will dress to glorify you; I will speak to glorify you; I will surround myself with the kind of friends that bring glory to your name. I will carefully and prayerfully see that my outward appearance represents the wonderful work of salvation you have wrought inside me.

I rejoice in you . . .
I observe all your wonderful miracles in my life and respond in joy. I find my fun, my pleasure, my purpose in life in my commitment to you. I let you whisper words of positive reinforcement into my mind and heart instead of the negative, destructive thoughts of Satan.

I am in high spirits . . .
I do not live on an emotional high, because emotions can plummet any minute. Instead, I live on a high plane spiritually knowing that my spirit attuned to yours will keep me steady

158

and consistent through all the emotional ups and downs of life. I live on a mountaintop spiritually, not because of me, but because of you and what you have done for me in Jesus. He gave me a life of freedom.

I sing praises to you, Lord . . .
With my mouth I give voice to the praises swelling within my heart. I sing in the spirit, I make melody to you in my heart. I worship you in private as well as when I am in worship with others.

You did not forget the cry of my heart when I was afflicted, poor and humble.
You answered my cries for help. You delivered me from those things which held me bound. You released me from the prison of self. You set me on firm ground and gave direction sure and straight.

In you I am now living free.

Read Psalm 9

God is saying to me:

Thoughts I'm having today:

I've shared with the Lord:

Further thoughts and prayers:

Quickened

Psalm 22:23-25

I worship you, Lord! I praise you, God!
You do not despise or abhor my affliction. . . .
I cannot help but stand in wonder at the times I have had to
come to you for help and forgiveness and you have never once
gotten impatient with me. You have never refused to accept
my confession of sin and repentance, nor withheld from me
forgiveness and cleansing. You have not once looked away
from me in disgust. You do not look down upon my shortcomings as if I were an inferior creation. You have never told
me that I was too dirty or soiled to come into your presence.
Instead, you have openly invited me to come just as I am,
hiding nothing, but rather holding everything before you for
your examination and cleansing.
You have not hid your face from me. . . .
Whenever I have needed you, I have found you there waiting,
ready to help me. I have not had to go looking for you, coaxing
you to come and reveal yourself to me. Any time that I was not
able to see you, it was because my own vision was obscured
and veiled, but when I choose to see you, you are there.
When I prayed and cried to you, you heard. . . .
You are not deaf. You hear even my faintest cry. When I cry to
you, you hear me. When I remember to pray, instead of complain, I am sure of having your ear.
Praise your name forever!
I eat and am satisfied. . . .
You are truly the bread of life. With this provision, my spirit is
fully satisfied. I drink of you and my thirst is continually
quenched.
I diligently seek for, inquire of and for Him. . . .
My life is spent in searching out the deep recesses of the almighty God. I am continually in wonder about the involve-
ment of the Most High in the lives of His humble children. I
search His Word and find answers to my questions. I stand on

His wonderful Word and find solutions to all my problems.

He is found. . . .

God is not an elusive dream or phantom to chase, but a divine person to know. He does not avoid us, but seeks us. When we seek Him, the contact is instantaneous.

He is my greatest need. . . .

I think I need food, but I need God more. I think I need money, but He has riches for me that money cannot buy. I think I need identity, when in knowing Him, my identity is found. I need love, and He is love expressed to me in Jesus without reserve. I need to give love, and He receives it gladly. I need recognition and He calls me His child.

My heart is quenched now and shall remain quickened forever, quickened to live free.

Read Psalm 22

God is saying to me:

Thoughts I'm having today:

I've shared with the Lord:

Further thoughts and prayers:

Expecting and Waiting

Psalm 27:1, 14

The Lord is my light and my salvation;
I am not afraid of anyone. . . .
The Lord is the one that gives direction to my path. No matter what the situation, I know that He will rescue me. He gives me understanding and insight into spiritual things. He reveals himself to me through His Word. I have seen His hand move in my behalf for needs and demands of this life. I am dependent on Him. I am completely free from the fear of man. I am not intimidated by those with greater education. The wealthy do not have more than I have in Jesus. I am not overly impressed by celebrities, nor unduly swayed by men of influence. I can ask for advice or counsel on a decision and still remain objective. I am not pressured to compromise because of what others may think of me. Because He has made me strong, I am released from fear.

The Lord is my refuge and stronghold.
I am no longer afraid. . . .
My security for the future is in the Lord, not in insurance policies, not in my own accomplishments. I have positive direction to my life as I live out His divine will for me. I have a definite sense of security about the things of the future and of eternity. The fears that once held me in their grip are gone. They were part of my old life. As a new creature in Christ I am living free from fear. I am safe in Jesus.

I wait for and hope for and expect the Lord. . . .
I don't spend my time whistling in the dark, hoping for morning. Instead, I actively spend my time and energy in supplication to God. I make my petitions known to Him, and then pray without ceasing as He reveals His will in a matter to me. I pray in accordance with His Word, learn to be patient, and move in His timing. In waiting for and hoping in the Lord, I live in expectancy, not anxiety.

I am brave and I am of good courage. . . .
I may not be brave without tears, but am brave in spite of
tears. I don't expect to be without any apprehensions, but can
expect to move ahead in the face of them. I have courage because He strengthens me to do what is right.

My heart is stout and enduring. . . .
I have learned to endure, perseverance has become a part of
me. I am made strong through my trials and temptations. I
will not faint in the face of trouble, but will conquer.

As I wait for and hope for and expect the Lord . . .
I am learning valuable lessons of faith. By waiting for and
expecting the Lord, I live in more freedom every day.

Read Psalm 27

God is saying to me:

Thoughts I'm having today:

I've shared with the Lord:

Further thoughts and prayers:

Praise and Dependence

Psalm 34

I choose to bless the Lord at all times. . . .
My praises to Him are my offering to Him. I choose to bless
the Lord with my worship and praise in the good times and the
hard times.

His praise is continually in my mouth. . . .
The word constantly on my tongue shall be that of praise. I
don't have to complain and cry with despair . . . I can have instead constant praise and blessing to the Lord on my lips.

My life makes its boast in the Lord. . . .
My life shall be a testimony of what the Lord has done. My
victories are really His victories. My power to overcome is
none other than His own power. He gives me the armor and
ammunition to fight and win—the glory is all His. I have nothing to boast of except Jesus.

*I want my distressed and discouraged friends to hear me
and take courage for themselves. . . .*
God does not favor me above others. Those closest to me know
of the struggles I face almost daily in my own life. Victory by
its very definition implies a foregone battle, but I can be assured of my position with the victor because of the blood Jesus
shed in my behalf. No one need be left out of this victory in
Christ.

*O magnify the Lord with me, let's exalt His name to-
gether. . . .*
Let's share the goodness of the Lord, and experience the
strength and unity of worshiping Him together. There is something special about praising the Lord together for what He is
doing in each other's lives. We share our joys and victories,
and are not alone in them. Let us raise our voices as one to a
God who is worthy of all our praise.

Praise the Lord!

I sought for the Lord. . . .

I looked for His hand in every situation of my day. I sought for His working in my heart and attitudes. I sought His will for every decision, looking to Him for the solution to every cloud of trouble. I expected the strength of His Holy Spirit in the face of adversity. I searched His Word for help and guidance.

I required of Him. . . .

My life is submitted completely to His will and purpose, so I waited for clear orders from Him as to the direction to take. I stood firm on His promises. I ordered my day according to His Word, and expected His faithfulness.

He answered me. . . .

He gave me direction, He gave me hope, He gave me purpose, He sent me in the right way . . . He supplied my needs, and He spoke to me throughout the day.

He delivered me . . .

He sent relief and restoration. He gave mercy and forgiveness, always available because of His sacrifice on the cross. He has loosed me from bondage, and calls me by name, claiming me for His own. He forgives my sins, and overlooks my inabilities, giving me His own righteousness and strength.

I shall not lack any beneficial thing . . .

He does and will supply all my needs. He knows what is best for me and I can trust Him for all that is good.

I tell Him my needs . . .

I can freely share with Him all my needs, and He gently helps me discern between needs and desires.

I stand on His Word . . .

Nothing in this world is worth standing on, except His Word. He gives me the necessary courage to stand firm, waiting for Him to do what He has promised.

He answers my prayers. . . .

My hopes are all fulfilled in Jesus. I can actually see the hand of God move in the circumstances that threaten to overwhelm me. I can see His protecting force in the situations that would otherwise conquer me. He gives me clear and complete direction. He gives me assurance . . . I don't have to guess about the answers.

God is present, is all for me, and because of this, I *live free.*

Read Psalm 34

God is saying to me:

Thoughts I'm having today:

I've shared with the Lord:

Further thoughts and prayers:

Trust in God

Psalm 62:8

I trust in God . . .
I have a firm belief in His honesty, reliability and trustworthi-
ness. My hope is in Him; I have no misgivings; I expect Him to
meet all my needs as I yield and surrender to Him.

I lean on Him . . .
I rest the entire weight of my life's burdens, situations, circumstances, and decisions on Him. I do not lean on my own
understanding, but always choose to trust in the understanding and insight that He gives me.

I rely on the Lord . . .
I depend on Him. When I pray and surrender a situation to
Him, I no longer take matters into my own hands or try to figure them out for myself apart from Him and His Word. I am
entirely open to Him and find that He is entirely merciful and
loving to me, even when He corrects me.

I have confidence in Him at all times . . .
I have seen firsthand His power and might loosed in support of
His children. I know through His miraculous workings in my
own heart and in my home that He can be depended upon for
every problem we face. I have discovered His mighty love for
me and readiness to manifest His power consistent with my
varied needs.

I can pour out my heart before Him . . .
He will not criticize me for not having more faith . . . He will
teach me how to build it. He will not taunt me for being out of
control . . . He will teach me to take control. He will not scold
me for wrongdoing . . . He will forgive me. He will not accuse
me of faithlessness . . . He will demonstrate His faithfulness.
He will not chastise me for being weak . . . He will build
strength within me. He will not laugh at me . . . He will love
me.

He is a refuge for me . . .
A place for me to hide in safety.
He is my fortress . . .
A place of protection and strength.
He is my strong tower . . .
My centurion . . . My guard.

How can I help but love Him? He gives me all that I need to *live free.*

Read Psalm 62

God is saying to me:

Thoughts I'm having today:

I've shared with the Lord:

Further thoughts and prayers:

Safe Home and Free

Psalm 91

I dwell . . .
Live, reside, abide, repose, rest, relax—in familiar surroundings. I am very comfortable with Him, totally at home.

In the secret place . . .
No enemy can find me here. This is God's secret place. It is the center of His will—secure and safe. This is God's hideaway for me from the world, the flesh, and the devil. The world looks at me and wonders how I can live in this calm when all around me is turmoil. How can I have a confidence in the future when all the signs seem so uncertain? Because I live in the place held secret to all except those who live in God.

Of the most high . . .
The Almighty God. The Everlasting Father. The Prince of Peace. The living, true God. The one who is above all others, and by whom all things were made. He is the Alpha and Omega, the Creator of the Universe. The one who gave His own son for my sins, MY FATHER.

I remain . . .
I stay, unmoved, fixed forever.

Stable . . .
I no longer sway in direction, purpose or desire. I am emotionally stable, spiritually and physically fit. I am rooted and grounded, I have sure footing.

Under the shadow . . .
Very close to, even united with the Father, I am sheltered from the blinding blasts of life's realities and given insight into the realities of eternity. I am protected from the onslaughts of the accuser, and experience the mercies of the Father. He gives relief from the weight of sorrow with His words of comfort. I am relieved from all pressures by His complete rest.

Of the Almighty . . .
God himself—here present, close to me. Not some distant, vague hope of help, but a Father who is all-powerful, all-

loving, all-caring, all-wise and all-present—waiting to hear me call upon Him.

Living as He planned, I am *living free.*

Read Psalm 91

God is saying to me:

Thoughts I'm having today:

I've shared with the Lord:

Further thoughts and prayers:

Detach here

- -

For information regarding OVEREATERS VICTORIOUS and for current price lists on other materials, send a business-size, stamped, self-addressed envelope to Overeaters Victorious Inc., P.O. Box 179, Redlands, CA 92373.

If you would like to receive special mailings concerning Overeaters Victorious seminars in your area, fill out the form below.

Name _____

Address _____

City/State _____ Zip _____